Merry Christmas,
Mom
from Mikki
December 2000

Seasoned *with* Words

A COOKBOOK

STORIES,

MEMOIRS

&

POEMS

ABOUT

FOOD

OREGON WRITERS COLONY

COLONYHOUSE COLLECTION
VOLUME ONE

Published by Oregon Writers Colony, PO Box 15200, Portland, OR, 97292-5200.

Type set in New Baskerville
Designed by Donnelleigh S. Mounce
Illustrated by Joanne Mehl

Printed in the United States of America

ISBN 1-891535-01-3

Acknowledgements

This book was produced by an editorial board of seven writers, which we trust proves that too many cooks don't spoil the broth. Members of the editorial board: Marlene Howard, chair; Susan A. Bronson; Judith Massee; Martha Miller, recipe testing; Lynda Marie Nygaard; Sally R. Petersen, production; Kitty Purser. Others who helped include Elizabeth Bolton, who used her poet's sensibilities to create the sequence of these essays, memoirs and poems; Dorothy Brehm and Joleen Colombo who copy- and proofread; and Jean Bradley, who handled ISBN matters.

Contents

Seasoned *with* Words

A COOKBOOK

Let Us Break Bread Together

WE ENVISION THIS BOOK AS A COLLECTION of personal stories emphasizing the connection between each writer and food. From the beginning, the book's editorial board planned not just a collection of recipes, but an anthology focused on the writer's connection with food.

This is fitting for a cookbook sponsored by Oregon Writers Colony because the idea for the organization was created in a beach house kitchen. It was late spring in 1980 when Lola Janes and I drove to Arch Cape on the Oregon coast, to visit our friend Jean Auel whose first novel, *The Clan of the Cave Bear*, was now a best seller. The three of us had become friends in a writing class the previous summer.

That balmy evening Jean took time from working on her second novel to cook us a wonderful meal and open a couple of bottles of her special Neister Rhine wine. Way after midnight we talked about the group of writers we'd met in Don James' writing class and what an inspirational teacher Don was. He hadn't been invited to teach a class that summer, so we concluded that we should rent a place, invite ex-class members, and hold our own classes. We even created a name — the Don James Invitational Writing Conference. Easy enough to decide when you've just enjoyed three glasses of wine each.

"And I know the perfect place for the classes," Jean said. So, at 2:30 a.m. we walked down the road to peer into the windows of a large beach rental house called Casa Pacifica. We carefully wrote the rental telephone number on my hand because we had a pen but no paper with us.

The next day back in Portland I reserved the space for mid-October and we began making phone calls. Don James volunteered his enthusiastic support and gave me the phone numbers for his writer friends Walt Morey, author of *Gentle Ben*, and writer/teacher Nan Phillips. He told me to recruit both of them to speak. A call to Jean Auel confirmed that she could be with us, fresh from an author's tour for her book. We mailed letters and made phone calls to all the Don James class members. Nan Phillips taught writing classes at the coast for the community college, so she recruited some of her students to attend.

We drafted my husband, Spud Howard, to plan and serve the meals from his restaurant in Seaside. We sponsored a writing contest and gave two conference scholarships to the winners. Tom Birdseye, now a well-known Oregon children's author, won our first scholarship.

It was a glorious weekend. Twenty-eight of us ate, slept only a little, listened to the experts, and shared experiences with our contemporaries, always about writing and publishing. We began Friday evening and reluctantly left Sunday afternoon. In the wrap-up session everyone begged us to do this again soon.

"We need a place of our own to hold these conferences," I said. I was young then, and nothing was impossible.

Eight years later, in 1988, after Lola Janes had died of cancer, her husband, Sam, and Jean Auel gave us money toward the down payment on the Colonyhouse. I sent out 400 letters to everyone who had ever shown any interest in our project and we raised the final $5000.

In 1998 we celebrated our 10th anniversary of owning the Colonyhouse in Rockaway Beach on the Oregon coast. Through-out these 10 years, hundreds of writers have used the facility for critique groups, retreats, workshops, and classes.

Shared meals continue to be a part of Colonyhouse stays. Often the help a writer needs in solving a technical problem comes as conference participants work together in the kitchen assembling a meal or doing the dishes. We've shared characters, plots, queries, proposals, agent and editor gripes, celebrations of contracts and sales with each other at potlucks, barbecues, and picnics.

We've solved problems of conflict and premise over morning coffee and met each other in the kitchen raiding the refrigerator at midnight after we finally finished a 10 page rewrite. The Colonyhouse is there for us and we are thankful.

I wish to mention and remember Colony members who are no longer with us:

Lola Janes, who loved to sit around the fire, drink coffee and talk writing.

Don James, who gave us the original inspiration when he told us, "Writing is not a competitive sport. Give orchids to the living, your writing friends."

Walt Morey, the story-teller who kept us enthralled.

Nan Phillips, the master teacher, who believed in her students and never stopped teaching.

Tommy Thompson, the writer-producer who had gone to Hollywood, made good, but came back to Oregon to teach us to dream big dreams.

And to all the writers, teachers, students who have made this dream come true, I say, "Thank you."

———◆———

Marlene Howard is founder, past president, and member of Oregon Writers Colony.

Red Hot Papa

LOLA JANES LOVED LIFE. In 1983, when Oregon Writers Colony held an early conferences in Gearhart on the Oregon coast, Lola, a co-founder with Marlene Howard, could be seen talking earnestly with conferees and savoring every aspect of the gathering — the camaraderie, the writing experience, and the food! Her large brown eyes snapped with enthusiasm as she convinced new members that there was no better place in the world for them to be. In the evenings after the speakers and readers had spun themselves out, she gathered everyone around an old piano and sang familiar ballads way past midnight.

My husband Joe and I were in serious courtship at that time and our recollections of the early days at Gearhart are treasured pages in our album of memories. Romance, writing, and good food. Who could have wished for more!

Spud Howard was responsible for the group's cuisine. Barbecues, replete with artistically carved fruit, scrumptious salads, and rich desserts abounded, accenting the high that writers get after a day of stimulating interchange.

Chili was one of Spud's special dishes. He brewed pots of it while Lola and Marlene organized activities. One year Spud entered a statewide chili contest. Lola encouraged his efforts by fashioning him a red chef's hat. He didn't win, but he wore that hat proudly at many conferences thereafter.

Lola and Marlene were tireless in their efforts to seed Oregon Writers Colony and make it grow into a mecca for writers. I was among the first board members who witnessed in awe how much they gave of themselves. In 1985 when OWC had its plans for Colonyhouse underway, Lola was diagnosed with cancer. The months that followed were agonizing. She fought the disease with all her might, and her buoyant spirit seemed to hold it in abeyance for awhile. When her body began to give up, Lola's indomitable optimism prevailed until the end.

Lola died on July 24, 1987, a day before Joe and I were married — an oppressive cloud over one of the happiest days of our relationship — a day Lola would have loved to have celebrated with us.

Our homestyle wedding was everything we had planned. We said our vows under our 100-year-old beech tree. Among other friends, Marlene and Spud were part of the festivities. Marlene and her daughter, Denise, sang, and Spud added his culinary magic to the reception following the ceremony which we held outdoors, just as we had the early Oregon Writers Colony conference dinners. The tables were laden with fancy fruit, tasty salads, and, yes, steaming pots of the famous chili. And, wouldn't you know, Spud wore the red chef's hat on which Lola had embroidered RED HOT PAPA!

Spud's Chili

1 OR 2 (ACCORDING TO TASTE) SEEDED AND FINELY CHOPPED JALAPEÑO PEPPERS
1 LARGE ONION COARSELY DICED
3-4 CLOVES GARLIC FINELY MINCED

1 4-OUNCE CAN DICED GREEN CHILIES
1 28-OUNCE CAN CHOPPED TOMATOES
2 TABLESPOONS GROUND CUMIN SEED
2 TABLESPOONS CHILI POWDER
1 TEASPOON SALT
1 1-POUND BAG DRIED PINTO OR RED BEANS
1 POUND COARSE GROUND EXTRA LEAN BEEF

Put beans in a large cooking pan and cover with water. Lightly salt water and let soak overnight (or for a quick soak bring to a boil, remove from heat and let stand for 1 hour). Cook beans until soft, adding enough water to keep covered if necessary.

In a large stock pot brown the ground beef until medium rare then drain off fat. Add onions, garlic, green chilies and jalapeños. Simmer until onions are tender. Add cumin, chili powder and salt and simmer for about 2-3 minutes to allow flavors to meld. Add tomatoes and continue to simmer for 15-20 minutes, stirring often. Add beans with about half of the cooking water. Continue to simmer for about 30 minutes. Taste and correct seasonings. Serve with garnish of shredded cheddar cheese and chopped onions, if desired.

———————

Doreen Gandy Wiley artist, teacher, noted poet and photographer, makes her home in Portland, Oregon. She is the author of Fires of Survival, *a novel of life during the Japanese occupation of the Philippines in World War II.*

How Did You Learn
To Cook Like That?

M Y FAMILY LIVED ON A FARM in Northeastern Oregon, where we grew wheat and green peas. We lived next to my Grandpa and Grandma Howard and my Great Grandma Howard who moved out from Kansas to live with them after Great Grandpa passed away.

No kids my age lived closer than four miles so I spent most of my time with my mother and grandmothers. One of my earliest memories is sitting on the counter in my grandmother's large kitchen and helping my great grandma, who I called "little grandma," make noodles. My job was to watch as she mixed the dough, rolled it out and then cut it into noodles. My job was to separate the strands and lay them on a clean white dishtowel to dry. Try as I might, I still cannot duplicate the taste and texture or her chicken and noodles.

Every summer mom and my grandmother canned hominy, tomatoes, beans, pickled beets, pickled peaches, applesauce, sauerkraut, dill pickles, mustard pickles, jellies and jams. They "let me help" by picking and cleaning whatever was to be canned that day and by sitting on a stool out of the way and watching as they prepared and canned the food for the winter.

During pea harvest we roomed and boarded the 80 to 90 men required to run two 12-hour shifts seven days a week for about 30 days. My mom, grandma and a hired woman cooked for the crew. This harvest speed was necessary because green peas raised on dry land farming are easily damaged by heat. I remember one time we were harvesting and across the road was a field of four hundred acres that was to be next. A hot north wind started to blow and in three and a half hours the entire field was lost.

When I was 10 years old, my first real job began — peeling potatoes, washing dishes, cleaning the dining room, picking and cleaning vegetables from the garden, helping serve the meals, packing lunches and whatever else my mom told me to do. It paid a dollar a day and was hot, hard work, but today it is one of the many happy memories I have of living on the farm.

Just the taste and smell of my mother's mustard pickles brings back another memory, one of my father and me "sneaking" a late night snack of cheddar cheese, crackers and mustard pickles while we stood close to the wood stove in the kitchen during the cold winter evening. I often think of these things now whenever I am asked, "how and where did you, a *man*, learn this kind of cooking?"

Mom's Mustard Pickles

4-5 POUNDS PICKLING CUCUMBERS (THE MEDIUM SIZE WORKS BEST), WASHED
AND BLOSSOM STEMS REMOVED
1 GALLON WHITE VINEGAR
1 CUP PICKLING SALT (NON-IODIZED)
1 CUP WHITE SUGAR
1 CUP DRY YELLOW MUSTARD

In a stainless steel or glass (non-aluminum) pot mix the vinegar, salt, sugar and mustard. Bring to a boil stirring to dissolve the dry ingredients. Reduce heat and keep mixture hot. Pack cucumbers snugly into hot sterilized canning jars. Fill jar with hot liquid leaving ½" head space. Seal jars and process in a boiling water bath for 10 minutes. Place in a cool area. Pickles are ready to use in about two weeks. You may notice a sediment at the bottom of a jar after setting for a while. This is normal. You should have about 10-12 pints.

————————

Spud Howard, as he is known to intimate friends and chance acquaintances alike, from the beginning has fueled many Oregon Writers Colony gatherings with his good food.

An Idaho Legacy

DON JAMES BECAME THE CATALYST for a writers organization through the inspiration generated by his teaching. He taught writing classes at the Portland State University summer study program, Haystack, named for the offshore monolith near Cannon Beach, Oregon.

By leaving Don James off the list of invited teachers one summer, the school inadvertently brought Oregon Writers Colony into existence when a group of writers decided to organize a workshop around Don James' teaching. (see "Let Us Break Bread Together," p. 7.)

The writers knew James was a fine teacher; they also knew he loved "pasties." They were his favorite food all his life. When he attended college his grandmother sent him enough pasties to last the week for him and his impoverished veteran friend, Bill. He dearly loved his grandmother and even when he was very old he was still grateful to her for her kindness.

Miners took pasties into the mines. Butte, Montana, became famous for them. They were nostalgically called, "letters from home."

Butte Pasties (Irish)

Tips: Make all ingredients the size of the end of your little finger. Use at least 4 tablespoons butter. Crimp carefully with water to avoid leakage. Wrap cooked pasties in aluminum foil. Freeze. Heat in oven. (Great when cook is away from home and non-cook is alone.)

1/2 POUND RAW BEEF STEAK, DICED
1 CUP CHOPPED ONION
1 LARGE TABLESPOON BUTTER
1 CUP DICED RUTABAGAS (IF DESIRED)
1 MEDIUM SIZED POTATO, DICED
SALT AND PEPPER

PIE DOUGH
1 1/2 CUPS FLOUR (PASTRY)
1/2 TEASPOON BAKING POWDER

1/4 TEASPOON SALT
1/3-1/2 CUP SHORTENING (BUTTER OR OTHER FAT)
1/4 CUP COLD WATER (ABOUT)

Sift flour, salt and baking powder together; then mix as for pie dough, shape and roll as in directions below. (This recipe makes two pasties.)

For one pasty use one-half the dough. Roll thin into the shape and size of pie plate. Pile half the potato, onion, meat, and if desired, the rutabaga on only half the round of pie dough, and to within 1" from edge. Sprinkle with salt and pepper and dot with butter. Fold other half of this dough over this filling, press edges together well. Repeat process. Place two pasties in pie plate. Cut slit in top of each, into which a teaspoon of hot water should be poured occasionally to keep from drying out. Bake ³/₄ hour in hot oven (400°F) or until well browned, then reduce to 350°F for 15 minutes.

———————

The information and recipe were supplied by writer Florence Samuel, Don James' dear friend who learned to make the pasties for him. Samuel was a member of the organizing committee that first met to make plans for the organization which eventually became Oregon Writers Colony. The recipe originally came from Montana Sen. Mike Mansfield's wife. Mansfield and James corresponded occasionally for years. Florence Samuel assisted James in producing the Butte Memory Book. *She resides in Rockaway Beach, Oregon, and is compiling a* Don James Memory Book.

Clan of the Cave Bear

JEAN AUEL ALREADY HAD COMPLETED the manuscript for *Clan of the Cave Bear* and had a New York agent when she attended the 1979 Portland State University "Haystack" writing class taught by Don James.

Class members shared in the excitement when her agent phoned telling Jean she was auctioning her novel and needed two more copies of the manuscript. I'm not sure many in that class knew what a book auction was, but after that day we did.

The only phone at the school was outdoors, and class members remember huddling in the rain waiting to hear a report on every word of the conversation with a "real New York agent."

The rest is history, told where writers gather. Jean's Earth's Children series sold with the biggest book advance ever paid to an unknown author. *Clan of the Cave Bear* led the way to instant success and a fine writing career for Jean.

Her descriptions of the food and medicine used by the ancient ones represented amazing feats of research, some of it conducted outdoors, experimentally.

Here then, from the book that helped Oregon Writers Colony realize its dream of a writing haven, is a ritual feast as our ancestors might have cooked it.

The Feast

By late afternoon, delicious smells were drifting away from the several fires where food was cooking, and pervading the area near the cave. Utensils and other cooking paraphernalia that had been salvaged from their former cave and carried in the bundles by the women had been unpacked. Finely made, tightly woven waterproof baskets of subtle texture and design, created by slight alternations in weaving, were used to dip water from the pool and as cooking pots and containers. Wooden bowls were used in similar ways. Rib bones were stirrers, large flat pelvic bones were plates and platters along with thin sections of logs. Jaw and head bones were ladles, cups, and bowls. Birchbark glued together with balsam gum, some reinforced with a well-placed knot of sinew, were folded into shapes for many uses.

In an animal hide, hung from a thong-lashed frame set over a fire, a savory broth bubbled. Careful watch was kept to make sure the liquid didn't boil down too far. As long as the level of boiling broth was above the level reached by the flames, it kept the temperature of the skin pot too low to burn. Ayla watched Uka stir up chunks of the meat and bone from the neck of the bison that were cooking with wild onion, salty coltsfoot, and other herbs. Uka tasted it, then added peeled thistle stalks, mushrooms, lily buds and roots, watercress, milkweed buds, small immature yams, cranberries carried from the other cave, and wilted flowers from the previous day's growth of day lilies for thickening.

The hard fibrous old roots of cattails had been crushed and the fibers separated and removed. Dried blueberries they had carried with them and parched ground grains were added to the resulting starch that settled in the bottom of the baskets of cold water. Lumps of the flat, dark, unleavened bread were cooking on hot stones near the fire. Pigweed greens, lamb's-quarter, young clover, and dandelion leaves seasoned with coltsfoot were cooking in another pot, and a sauce of dried, tart apples mixed with wild rose petals and a lucky find of honey steamed near another fire.

Iza had been especially pleased when she saw Zoug returning from a trip to the steppes with a clutch of ptarmigan. The low-flying, heavy birds, easily brought down with stones from the marksman's sling, were Creb's favorite. Stuffed with herbs and edible greens that nested their own whole eggs, and wrapped in wild grape leaves, the savory fowl were cooking in a smaller stone-lined pit. Hares and giant hamsters, skinned and skewered, were roasting over hot coals, and mounds of tiny, fresh wild strawberries glistened bright red in the sun.

It was a feast worthy of the occasion.

— *from* Clan of the Cave Bear, *1980, Crown Publishers*

Jean M. Auel lives in Oregon, where she currenty is engaged in researching and writing the fifth novel in The Earth's Children series. She is a founding board member of Oregon Writers Colony.

Writing and Food
at the Sylvia Beach

SYLVIA BEACH OWNED THE BOOKSTORE that Ernest Hemingway and other famous literary expatriates frequented in the Paris of the 1920s and '30s. The name, and perhaps the ambience, have been transported to the Oregon coast. Partners Goody Cable and Sally Ford opened the Sylvia Beach Hotel in Newport, Oregon, March 15, 1987. Two weeks later Oregon Writers Colony (OWC) moved their spring conference to the hotel. Now, after 12 years, when things get hectic Manager Ken Peyton regales his staff with horror stories of that first weekend.

Through repetition, the story has gained a mythic tone. It begins . . . .

"The chef I'd hired had quit to work in Alaska on a fishing boat and the fill-in chef had a death in the family. Conference guests begin to arrive early, before the agreed upon check-in time, so I hadn't gotten my totally green staff briefed yet." Ken is a pretty laid-back guy, but as he gets into this story his jaw tenses and he grimaces as he remembers.

"I was downstairs in the kitchen trying to get my food planned for the Friday evening dinner and the staff kept calling me upstairs to answer attendees' questions."

Problems began to pile up, complaints such as the dorm room dwellers demanding security for their luggage because there were no locks on the dorm room doors and the security lockers hadn't arrived yet. The conference facilitators had assured him that shouldn't be a problem because OWC had booked all the rooms and there were no other guests in the hotel. After the dorm dwellers agreed to the lack of security, they still were unhappy because the dorm was not "decorated" like the other rooms.

So, up and down from basement to first floor to third floor went Ken. Finally he shut himself in the kitchen to produce the "gourmet" meals as advertised. No time for made-from-scratch creations. This weekend it was United Grocer's frozen entrees and desserts.

There is no elevator in the hotel and the guests scheduled for third floor rooms were sending down complaints as they tired out on the second floor landing.

Shared adversity did create bonds. OWC members, in spite of some complaints, fell in love with the Sylvia Beach Hotel. After all, it is a book lover's paradise: no telephones or TVs in the rooms, a third floor study and library with coffee, tea, and mulled wine each evening. Each room is decorated to focus on the life and work of a specific author — from Agatha Christie and E.B. White on the first floor up past the Collette and Mark Twain rooms to the third floor Herman Melville — 22 rooms, plus two dorms.

OWC returns each spring and now everything runs smoothly. Charlotte Dinoit, assistant manager since 1988, greets conference attendees as old friends. Carole York, the dinner waitress for 10 years, is dressed to complement the meal theme as she welcomes attendees in the "The Tables of Content" dining room.

In 1991 OWC forged an additional bond with Sylvia Beach Hotel when the organization decorated the big dorm room. Rae Richen chaired the project during her OWC presidency. She solicited names of deserving Oregon writers from writing groups all over the state, then recruited an artist to paint murals honoring those chosen. Jean Auel, Don James, M.K. Wren, and Shannon Applegate are the OWC members and teachers who are included in these murals.

Chef Cathy Lusk, who has been with Sylvia Beach for more than 10 years, contributed some of our favorite recipes. All are from scratch, no mixes or frozen emergency fare here.

Gazpacho (Sylvia Beach)

2 CUCUMBERS PEELED AND CUT INTO1" SLICES
1 GREEN BELL PEPPER CORED AND CUT INTO LARGE CHUNKS
1 RED BELL PEPPER CORED AND CUT INTO LARGE CHUNKS
1 MEDIUM ONION PEELED AND CUT INTO LARGE CHUNKS
2 CLOVES GARLIC, PEELED
1 TABLESPOON SALT (MORE OR LESS TO TASTE)
1 TABLESPOON CHILI POWDER
1/3 TEASPOON GROUND CUMIN
1/3 TEASPOON GROUND CAYENNE PEPPER (MORE OR LESS TO TASTE)
1/2 CUP OLIVE OIL
1/4 CUP LEMON JUICE (2 LEMONS)
1 BUNCH CILANTRO, WASHED AND STEMS BELOW LEAVES REMOVED
35 OUNCES TOMATO JUICE
1/2 CUP CHOPPED OLIVES
3 GREEN ONIONS SLICED VERY THIN ON THE DIAGONAL

In food processor fitted with metal blade, puree the first 5 ingredients in small batches until chopped evenly into very fine pieces (not liquefied) Transfer to a large non-aluminum bowl or pot. Add the tomato juice. Whisk in the salt, chili powder, cumin and cayenne pepper to taste. Whisk in the olive oil and lemon juice. Cover and chill for several hours or overnight to allow flavors to blend.

Before serving, coarsely chop the cilantro and stir into the soup. Garnish with the chopped olives and green onions. Optional garnish: fresh shrimp stirred into the soup or served on the side. Serves 8.

Chocolate Poppers

ALMOND BROWNIES
8 OUNCES UNSWEETENED CHOCOLATE
12 OUNCES BUTTER
7 EGGS
1/2 TEASPOON SALT
1 1/2 TEASPOONS ALMOND EXTRACT
2 CUPS BLANCHED ALMONDS, GROUND
3 CUPS SUGAR
2 TABLESPOONS ESPRESSO POWDER

Melt chocolate and butter together. Cool slightly. Stir sugar into the chocolate mixture. Beat eggs one at a time into the chocolate mixture. Stir in the salt, almond extract, ground almonds and espresso powder. Do not overmix. Pour mixture into 13x19" pan that has been buttered and floured. Bake at 350°F until mixture is set up — it will be fudgey in the center. It is most important not to overbake!

Cut the cooled brownie into small circles (a donut hole cutter works well) and pipe buttercream frosting on each circle. Serves about five poppers per person.

BUTTERCREAM FROSTING
6 LARGE EGG YOLKS
3/4 CUP SUGAR
1/2 CUP CORN SYRUP

1 POUND BUTTER — SOFTENED AND LIGHTLY WHIPPED WITH A FORK
1/2 TEASPOON ALMOND EXTRACT
1/2 TEASPOON VANILLA EXTRACT
6 OUNCES BITTERSWEET CHOCOLATE, MELTED

Beat egg yolks with electric mixer until light in color. In small saucepan, combine corn syrup with sugar. Heat, stirring constantly until it reaches a full boil and immediately transfer to a glass measure cup. Using an electric mixer, beat the syrup into the egg yolks, being careful not to drop the syrup onto the beaters. Continue beating the mixture until it cools to the same temperature as the softened butter, (about 5 minutes).

Beat the softened butter by tablespoons into the cooled mixture. You should end up with smooth mixture. If it curdles, it means that your butter is too cool or your egg mixture is too warm. To remedy: Stir your mixture over a bowl of ice water just until it smooths out. Immediately remove from ice and beat in the remaining butter. Stir the almond and vanilla extracts and melted chocolate into the butter mixture.

Store at room temperature, do not refrigerate. This will hold for at least 2 days.

———————

Marlene Howard is founder, past president, and member of Oregon Writers Colony.

I Am Not Allowed to Attend Without It

WHEN MY BROTHER-IN-LAW MARRIED the first of three times, it was to a tall streamlined singer of folk music and jazz. Her voice was low and husky, her eyes large and dark, her chestnut hair touched her slim hips in back.

My clearest memory of her is a photo in which she resembles the Hollywood version of a heroine "squaw" — a fringed leather skirt dropping to calves encased in soft leather boots, a fringed vest that ended six inches above the hip hugging waist of her skirt leaving a lean stretch of tanned skin between the two. Silver buckles and turquoise jewelry weighed her down. On one hip she balanced a blond, blue-eyed two year old. Her other arm hugged the expanding waist of her wild-haired husband.

Marsha loved to cook; you could tell by looking at her husband. She subscribed to Bon Appetit! and read it like I read the Oregon Writers Colony Colonygram. I had no greater joy when visiting my husband's family in California than to watch her skim through the magazine, pick out a recipe, and whip up (quite literally) a souffle, a cream pie that stood several inches tall, or a double chocolate cake with German chocolate frosting. In the 10 years she was part of the family, I never saw her eat more than a taste of any of her creations, while I . . . .

Well, Marsha may have left our family, but she hasn't left my memory or my recipe box. Her hot pepper jelly, poured over an 8-ounce block of cream cheese and accompanied by small crispy wheat crackers, wins raves from young and old. I'm not allowed to attend family parties without it. Bon appetit!

Hot Pepper Jelly

3 LARGE BELL PEPPERS (2 RED, 1 GREEN)
1 TABLESPOON CAYENNE PEPPER (2 TEASPOONS FOR MILDER)
1½ CUPS CIDER VINEGAR
6 CUPS SUGAR
1 BOTTLE LIQUID PECTIN

Wash and remove seeds from peppers, grind in blender. Add cayenne and ¾ cup vinegar. Whirl until well chopped. Pour into large sauce pan with rest of vinegar and sugar. Bring to rolling boil, stirring constantly. Boil 5 minutes. Remove from heat. Cool 2 minutes. Add pectin and stir well. Pour into jars and cap with canning rings and lids. Tighten! Turn upside down to cool and seal. Makes 4-6 pints.

P.S.: I have successfully used powdered pectin, but it is added while on the stove. Read directions for berry jelly.

P.P.S.: Peppers can be any combination. I usually throw in some jalapeños.

P.P.S.S.: Jelly can be dyed with red food coloring.

————

Bonnie Bean Graham — past cook, past baker, past canner and jelly-maker. Now grandmother, now traveler, now writer and reveler.

Two Sisters' Sourdough Adventures

M Y SISTER LOIS AND I ONCE COMPILED and tested recipes for a sourdough cookbook. Not knowing a lot about the subject, we learned as we went. We conducted our experiments on kitchen counters — she at her house, I at mine. We had to make a "starter," grown from water and flour. I added a dash of sugar, feeding it to keep it going.

My starter bubbled and then oozed down the front of my cabinet drawers. It developed red and black spots and looked too alive for my taste.

Lois didn't get the same results, but then she was in a new house, I was not. I had a damp, dark, last-frontier basement that opened into my kitchen. Bacteria floated all over the place, making it the perfect place for sourdough experiments.

The book was printed, but I will tell you we don't care much for sourdough, and never made it again.

Not to worry, I have a super easy recipe that contains no sourdough and which will make everyone envious — looks like you worked all day. These freeze well and are great for parties.

Miniature Cheese Cakes

1 PACKAGE OF VANILLA WAFERS
1 CAN OF PIE FILLING SUGGESTED. CHERRY OR BLUEBERRY ARE BEST.
2 8-OUNCE PACKAGES OF CREAM CHEESE (NOT REDUCED FAT)
1 CUP SUGAR
2 EGGS
1 TEASPOON VANILLA

Line 24 muffin pan cups with fancy paper muffin cup liner, put a vanilla wafer in the bottom. Blend cream cheese, sugar, eggs and vanilla on medium speed of mixer until light and fluffy. Fill the cups ⅔ full. Bake at 325°F for 20 minutes. Do not brown. Cool and fill rest of way up with pie filling. I like to add a dollop of whip cream on top just before serving.

Irene Emmert is an Oregon Writers Colony (OWC) board member, past recording secretary and present historian. She is represented in two volumes of OWC's anthology, In Our Own Voices. *She writes a weekly news column for the Molalla Pioneer, Molalla, Oregon.*

I Prefer Mine Without the Mouse

M Y GRANDFATHER, R.W. (Pappy) Hendricks, was famous (some would say infamous) for his dandelion wine. Once when I was a kid, a mouse got into one of Pappy's crocks of fermenting wine. He told my mother that he had thrown out that batch, but she couldn't be sure that he really had. She always wondered if the jug of brew he gave her was some of the mouse wine. Pappy figured the fermentation process would take care of any bad stuff from the mouse. I don't know that I'd have taken his word for it though.

I don't have Pappy's original recipe. He, like me, wouldn't have followed a recipe exactly anyway. Here's one adapted from a couple of cookbooks. I myself haven't tried to make dandelion

wine, but I asked my winemaker friends, Dick and Mary Ferraro, to study this recipe and see if it looks feasible. They said it does. Let me know if it works. If you are kind enough to share any samples, I prefer mine without the mouse.

Dandelion Wine

When the sun is shining, pick enough UNSPRAYED DANDELIONS to make a GALLON OF BLOSSOMS. Pour a GALLON OF BOILING WATER over the blossoms and let the whole thing stand until the blossoms rise, about two or three days. Add the RINDS OF 3 ORANGES and 1 LEMON CUT FINE. Boil the mixture for 15 minutes, then strain it through cheesecloth or flannel. Add to the strained liquid 3 POUNDS OF SUGAR and the PULP OF THE ORANGES AND LEMON. When the mixture is lukewarm, add 2 TABLESPOONS OF DRY YEAST and stir. To keep the mice out, cover the mixture with a loose lid. (If the lid is too tight, though, the wine might explode. That happened once in Pappy's closet.)

Stir the brew three or four times a day until it starts to ferment, then let it sit for two or three more weeks. Strain the wine again before you bottle it. Cork the wine tightly and keep it in a cool, dark place. Your wine should be ready to drink now. If it turns out not to be suitable for social occasions, you can use it as an antidote for liver and kidney complaints.

— Excerpted from the manuscript
A Little Book of Oldtime Receipts: Some for Reading,
Some for Remembering, Some for Cooking,
to be published by Tamarack Books, Inc.

Susan Butruille is the author of Women's Voices from the Mother Lode, *published this fall,* Women's Voices from the Western Frontier, *a 1996 Oregon Book Awards finalist in literary nonfiction, and* Women's Voices from the Oregon Trail, *a 1993 regional bestseller. Susan's award-winning monthly column, "Women's Voices Past and Future," appears in the Portland-based Women's Journal. Her articles have appeared nationally and she has edited publications in the needle arts and in training and development.*

Wily

A hundred thousand parachutes
were floating on the breeze
The dandelion's airborne troops
— my garden's enemies!
But in my swinging hammock,
I was lying at my ease,

And, scribbling some lines of verse
as if I didn't care,
I seized the rhymes as they came by
like parachutes on air.
Invasions! Oh, it could be worse:
they bring a beauty rare,

And privately I have to smile
at my capitulation:
Defeat but seems, and in my guile
there's, secretly, elation:
I have these lines, and in a while
when flags of the conquering nation,

A thousand golden-headed flowers
are camping on my lawn
I'll rise, at leisure, with my shears,
a basket, and a yawn,
Behead each one, and spend some hours
simmering the dears.

For I will have this summer sun
distilled and pure and fine
And celebrate the battle won
in dandelion wine.

*Elizabeth Bolton lives on a hilltop farm in the woods above the
Columbia River. Her work reflects various careers — as teacher of
acting, as director of a children's camp, as farm wife and mother,
and as incurable poet and writer. She finds it hard to be this brief!*

How to Write a Damn Good Recipe

W HEN ASKED to produce a recipe for this book, the fiery Jim Frey, author of *How to Write a Damn Good Novel*, reverted to form and shouted, "Writers don't do projects. They write, damnit!"

For years Frey has traveled from California to lead popular critique and writing sessions at the Colonyhouse. Many Oregon Writers Colony writers learned their craft in the Frey workshops. The sessions became so popular that, while pulling newcomers from around the country, they also drew participants back for more.

Therefore his students have been not only Freyed, but Refreyed, and a handful of them Deep Freyed. They know how to write a damn good novel and all the Freying is beginning to pay off as Frey students begin to sell their work. So, they come back for more Freying several times a year, meeting at Colonyhouse to perfect their skills in novel writing. Here are their comments about Jim and his recipe, which he e-mailed to the editorial board following unrelenting pressure.

Writer's Tea

Take one tea bag, any flavor, put it in boiling water and drink. (I don't have time to screw around with anything more complicated than this.) — *James N. Frey*

You ask Jim for a RECIPE, and of course you're going to get CONFLICT, CONFLICT, CONFLICT. — *Marjorie Reynolds*

Of course, Jim would expect that some woman would boil the water and put in the tea bag for him. — *Sue Bronson*

Face it, if you're actually doing it, writing pages every day, you don't have much time to ding around with cooking, cleaning, sewing or getting laid. If it's a REAL writers cookbook it should address issues like how to avoid ever turning on an oven, how to reheat fried eggs and how to unwrap a candy bar one-handed. — *Gail McNally*

I tend to agree with Jim. When I'm writing my idea of a gourmet meal is to pop a TV dinner in the microwave and eat it without taking my fingers off the keyboard. It's not a pretty sight. What we writers all need is a wife. I've been trying to get Andy to consider a small surgery, but he remains firmly attached to his testosterone. So, until I complete my rewrite, it's "writer's tea" and T.V. dinners for me. — *Susan Clayton-Goldner*

Twenty-four hours minus seven for sleep is seventeen.

Seventeen minus eight for work and another one for driving is eight.

Take out an hour for shower, shave, general activities in the bathroom and. . .

I have seven left.

Take another hour out for general activity: walking from-to, picking up, putting down, cleaning, sharpening, poking and prodding. . . .

I'm left with six.

Spend two hours on household, spouse and kids (generosity here pays) and I have four left.

Give up a half hour to e-mail and I'm down to three and a half hours.

If I spend an hour reading in my genre, I have two and a half hours left to write (I cheat here by listening to books in the car). If I eat pre-packaged frozen food and edit while I eat, I can get in two hours of fiction writing a day.

My last novel took 2500 hours to write.

How the hell did he find the time to heat up the water?
— *Eric Witchey*

I'm surprised everyone doesn't see the obvious here. Jim has concocted an abiding metaphor for life. A bit Joycean rather than Hemingwayesque to be sure, but rich with old world symbolism, layered with clues to a deeper mystery, spiced with profound simplicity. I think I'll use it as the premise for my next novel.
— *Mitch Luckett*

Don't try to kid us, Jim Frey, you can't boil water.
— *Marlene Howard*

But he doesn't even drink tea. — *Martha Miller*

What about maximum capacity? Jim says "put your characters in hot water and keep them there." So, when you reach the boiling point, take it to the extreme. Create a cup of instant gourmet coffee, hot chocolate or spiced apple cider, a cup of instant noodles or Jello, a cup o' instant noodle soup or frozen steamed vegetables. Hot tea may be satisfying to mild Oregonians, but instant anything else is off the bell curve. — *Linda Leslie*

Jim's cookbook entry is turning up the heat on the cookbook stew pot.

It got Marlene to throw something. Success: make "mild Oregonians" mad. Jim has created conflict, conflict, conflict. The ultimate mentor — wax on, wax off . . . tea bag boiled, tea bag burst.

May your fire burn and cauldron bubble. — *Rae Richen*

Jim Frey's authoritative book is How to Write a Damn Good Novel. *He hails from California, traveling north annually to teach intensive (and damn good) workshops at the Colonyhouse.*

Teacups

I TRACE THE PATH of my writing in the teacups lined up on my desk at the end of the day. The motley little train tells me how persistent I have been, how attentive to process, how deeply into the page I traveled before resurfacing. They are my link between the tangible world and the one I create, and an affirmation of my willingness to suspend my own disbelief.

A cup is something to hold as much as it is a vessel to drink from. A tactile connection between surface and soul. My kitchen shelves hold a varied assortment, collected mostly one at a time wherever I find them. They range from hefty pottery mugs, to delicate antique versions with intricate handles too small to insert a finger, to oriental tea bowls with no handles at all. As I write, I select them from the shelf without much conscious thought. So a new procession is created each day. Some days I grab what is nearest at hand. Other days I find myself rummaging in the back corners for something a bit more illusive.

The lineup always begins with "Big Blue" and a hearty brew of English Breakfast tea, Earl Grey, or Yorkshire blend. Blue is a rotund mug, painted in my favorite shade of periwinkle, that actually holds two cups. It is the perfect size and shape to cradle in two hands, warming them on those cold winter mornings, not all of which come in winter. Big Blue is my mantra to the muse, my touchstone of faith, and my earthly comfort.

On a good day, I don't get to the bottom of Big Blue. Somewhere in the process of sipping and rocking the writing takes over. A word, a sentence, a paragraph, a page later, the cold, neglected tea jolts me into going downstairs and brewing a fresh batch. On a really good day, I don't see the bottom of any of the cups that follow.

All this doesn't have as much to do with consuming tea as it does with ritual. As I absentmindedly trail down the stairs, warm the kettle, and select a new cup, the process of writing continues. Five minutes of pacing while the tea steeps can clarify an idea, bring just the right word to mind, or tune an inner ear to the voice of a fictional character.

After the warmup breakfast tea, what goes into the entourage is as varied as the cups themselves. Finding a new blend of tea is like finding a new story to tell; each connects us to something else. It might be a green tea from the Orient, a tangy blend of fruit and spice, or the subtle coolness of lime flowers. The shelf holds a world of possibilities. When I need more than five minutes brewing time to mull things out, the garden awaits with its offerings of fresh basil, sage, chamomile, and mint.

Now I admit, leaving a trail of teacups scattered around the computer is a messy business. The practical thing to do would be to take the first one down with me when I go for a refill. The same thought process would occur; the same ritual would be honored. But the idea rarely occurs to me until later, and when it does, I know I have stepped back out of the page. Besides, if I did that, I would miss all the stories the cups have to tell.

Tips for Brewing Tea

Start with spotlessly clean utensils. That brownish haze on the inside of your favorite cup is tannin residue. It will add an undesirable, bitter taste.

Use cold, good tasting water. Let the tap run briefly before filling the kettle, use filtered water, or bottled spring water.

Do not use water that has been previously boiled. Water that has been left standing loses its oxygen and produces a flat-tasting cup of tea.

Use the correct ratio of tea, water and brewing time. Check each package; directions vary with the type of tea. The rule of thumb is one slightly-rounded teaspoon of tea, or one tea bag, for each six-ounce cup of water.

Pour the heated water over the tea bag, or infuser, just as it starts to boil. Cover the cup and let steep for three to five minutes. Use a timer; excess brewing time produces bitter tea.

For herb tea use one teaspoon of dried or two to three teaspoons of fresh herbs for each cup. Let steep for five to seven minutes. Fresh leaves should be bruised for better flavor.

Using this as a baseline, experiment to discover your own taste preferences by altering the amount of tea or water.

Add milk, lemon, sugar, or honey if you must, but sipping tea is about learning to enjoy subtlety and nuance in a moment of leisure.

Lemon Tea Bread

1³/₄ CUPS FLOUR
³/₄ CUP SUGAR
2 TEASPOONS BAKING POWDER
2 TEASPOONS FRESH LEMON ZEST
¹/₂ TEASPOON SALT
1 EGG
³/₄ CUP MILK
¹/₄ CUP VEGETABLE OIL
1 TABLESPOON FRESH LEMON JUICE

Preheat oven to 350°F. Grease two 6x3x2" loaf pans. Stir together flour, sugar, baking powder, lemon zest, and salt in a mixing bowl; set aside. Beat together egg, milk, oil, and lemon juice in another mixing bowl. Add flour mixture to liquid mixture all at once. Stir just until moistened. Divide batter between the two loaf pans. Bake at 350°F for 40-45 minutes. Remove from oven and let sit in pans for 10 minutes. Remove from pans; cool thoroughly on rack. Makes two small loaves.

———————

Jessica Wade is a freelance writer whose articles and short stories have appeared in newspapers and magazines. A naturalist at heart, historian by compulsion, her favorite topics are plants, wildlife, and gardening.

The Writer in the Kitchen

WRITING IDEAS COME UNSOLICITED. They float upward like an old cork bobber released from gravel by the nudge of an inquiring bottom feeder, I think.

My inspirations generally show up when I'm engaged in a physical, repetitive, usually boring, activity. Ironing (remember ironing?). Showering. Preparing long, complicated soups. Julia Child's French onion soup is great for inspiration. So is the split pea soup below. Both require advance preparation, a flame-red Belgian cast iron soup pot, chopping, assembling, and time.

The problem with mid-soup inspiration is that your hands are busy. Half the time they're greasy as well. A writer with an idea and busy, greasy hands is pitiful. Decisions and priorities, both terminally uncreative, must be made. Will the idea keep? Or must you stop NOW and write it down?

Leaving the kitchen for the office and computer is out of the question. After all, there's inspiration to soup also, and it carries its own imperative to be finished. Besides, the idea is not fleshed out enough for the computer.

Jot. That's the word. I need to jot the idea, quickly, before it's gone. I look around the kitchen while continuing to chop. Is there a nearby writing instrument and paper? Come on, we're in the kitchen, after all. Grocery lists take pencils and paper. Where are they? Wherever they've gone, they're not visible. I could use the tape recorder, it's voice-activated. It's also in the car at the moment, ready for inspiration en route to somewhere.

So back with more urgency to the decision: will the idea keep? Can I continue to develop it while chopping? Or will that little cork of an idea just keep on bobbing down my stream of consciousness and disappear? (Now that's a nice little followup to a pretty good simile. Almost enough to sidetrack me from the first idea onto a second one. I'm entering dangerous territory here.)

I decide to keep the first idea alive while speeding through the last soup steps. No one's around, I'll talk this idea through aloud. I'll try not to let it get too complex too fast. That will help me do two things at once. So I become a decision-making writer with busy hands talking to herself. Thank heavens I spend my days alone!

Here's the soup that makes it all possible.

Nancy's Split Pea Soup

3-4 POUNDS HAM HOCKS (SKINNED)
1 POUND PACKAGE SPLIT PEAS
1 CARROT
1 ONION
3 STALKS CELERY
1 TURNIP
1 BUNCH PARSLEY
1 LEEK
SALT AND PEPPER TO TASTE

Put ham and peas in cold water to cover, skim, and simmer 3 hours. Add chopped vegetables and parsley tied in a bunch. Simmer another hour and remove parsley. Remove ham from hocks; discard bones and excess fat. Run all or part of this through the blender if desired.

———————◆———————

Sally Petersen has just learned that Oregon Writers Colony board positions are held for life. When not attending writers' functions, she runs a solo business, The Write Touch, in Portland, Oregon, and writes essays, occasionally winning an award.

The Wereyam

W HEN THE CLOYING ODOR of scorched marshmallow and hot yam filled the greenhouse, Bill Mauer cursed softly. Another damned premature. He got up from his watchman's cot.

The light of the full moon gleamed on the glass walls, throwing ghostly shadows over a jungle of yam vines as high as his head. He could see nothing, but the smell of hot candied yam grew stronger by the second.

Sighing, Bill picked up his auto-rooter. Nothing to do but find the premature and dig it out before the yam burst and let the bad strain of nanocritters contaminate the whole patch.

Bioengineered self-cooking yams had made his fortune.

Self-cookers let even the busiest houseperson serve his/her family with nutritious meals with all of the rich goodness of genuine home cooking. But somehow the new, improved yams with the automatic self-candying option just weren't working out. He should have known better than to buy his yam nanotechnology from a firm calling itself "WerTech Transformations."

As Bill walked down the shadowy corridor sniffing out the premature, yam plants rustled in the wind, their dry leaves scratching against the glass walls. Now a yam runner caught around Bill's ankle, and he bent over to unwrap it.

Wait a minute. There's no wind *inside* the greenhouse.

Spooked, Bill ripped the yam loose, but a dozen others gripped his other ankle. He kicked viciously, but more and more vines clutched at his arms and legs. He tried to scream, but a burning hot candied yam thrust through his lips, cramming itself into his mouth and choking off the air.

A sharp yam stem plunged into his jugular, and a hot wave of pain struck as tiny nanocritters surged through his arteries, multiplying in their millions, transforming every protein, every molecule of his body. His arms and legs withered away, and his torso grew large, globular, yam shaped.

And now Bill, for the first time in his life, understood yams. He understood the softness of the mothering soil. He understood sunshine, the feel of rain, gentle as butterflies' wings, upon yam leaves. But most of all, he understood yam pain, the brutal heat of an oven, the steel of a knife slashing through the skin.

Now he understood forks.

He understood cruel white teeth tearing at the tender yellow flesh, and all the degrading vocabulary of man's inhumanity to yams. Rage flowed through his body, white, screaming anger. He felt a thirst for vengeance which must be satisfied, and could only be satisfied with blood, enough blood to drown centuries of oppression, millennia of baked yams, boiled yams, on the side, yams with butter, yams with sour cream, and worse, yes, worse than all of those — candied yams.

Now the light of the full moon gleamed on the glass walls of the greenhouse. Bill's transformation was complete. Like a huge round moon he rolled to the greenhouse door, and a great rough beast, its hour come round at last, slouched towards the grocery stores to be born.

— *"The Wereyam" first appeared in The Magazine of Fantasy and Science Fiction*

Candied Yams

2-3 MEDIUM SIZED YAMS
BUTTER OR MARGARINE
3/4 CUP BROWN SUGAR
CINNAMON
NUTMEG
1 CUP SMALL MARSHMALLOWS

Slice yams into 2" thick rounds. Boil until soft (about 10-15 minutes). Peel off skins. Arrange yams in 8" square baking dish. Dot generously with butter or margarine. Sprinkle generously with brown sugar. Season to taste with cinnamon and nutmeg. Bake at 350°F until bubbly (about 20 minutes). Sprinkle marshmallows over top and continue baking until brown (about 5 minutes).

(We have photographic evidence of the author attending a dinner at which these yams were served. The horror, the horror!)

———————

Kent Patterson was a nationally known science fiction and fantasy writer from Eugene, Oregon, who before his death in 1995 achieved a small degree of infamy for his Tuber Tales, *including stories about an Idaho russet stampede, a potato-worshiping religious cult, and "The Wereyam" story accompanying this recipe, which was contributed by Kathy Oltion.*

Patterson's critique group met regularly at Colonyhouse. Unable to negotiate steps, Patterson was carried up a lengthy flight of external stairs on a straight chair lifted by friends. They later donated memorial funds in Kent's name. Oregon Writers Colony is exploring additional funding sources to investigate the feasibility of modifications that would make the house accessible to writers who have difficulties with mobility.

Beware the Barbarian –
Advice to Evil Wizards

I F YOU ARE A POWERFUL WIZARD with intentions of taking over/destroying the world, there are 10 things you absolutely must know.

1. No matter how powerful your magic, it will not be enough to stand against one pissed-off brawny-thewed barbarian with a sword. You can transform yourself into a dragon, hurl energy bolts, or turn invisible, and these won't help. If the barbarian gets inside your castle and close enough to carve you with his blade, you are history.

2. No matter how adept your palace guards are in swordplay, they will not be enough to stop the PO'd brawny-thewed barbarian. As a rule, barbarians go through guards like a tyrannosaur goes through a flock of sheep.

II. If the Captain of your Castle Guard, who is undoubtedly a master of some esoteric martial art, tells you he can handle the situation alone, you might as well buy him a coffin and arrange to send flowers to his wife. At best he will manage a superficial cut or three upon a few thews before the barbarian takes his head. Barbarians go through martial arts masters only slightly slower than they do guards.

3. If your most trusted advisor tells you that your magic and palace guards are more than enough to stop one lousy, stupid, ill-mannered barbarian, fire him and get yourself a new advisor.

4. If your new advisor throws the bones, reads the goat entrails and scrys the crystal and sees the teeny-tiniest bit of trouble even remotely connected to the barbarian, in any of his divinations, double his salary, then catch the next caravan leaving town.

II. This would be a good time to visit your brother-in-law at the Dread Sea for a couple of weeks. Wear a disguise, change your name, and take some sunblock. Barbarians are not known for their patience. By the time you come home, he will have moved on, provided you gave him no reason to stay. (See Rule #5, following.)

5. Do **not** kidnap the brawny-thewed barbarian's drop-dead gorgeous girlfriend to use as bait in the extremely foolhardy business of luring him into your castle. This will do naught but piss him off, and the last place you want him to be in that state of mind is in your castle. (See Rule #1.) If you must kidnap his girlfriend, have her transported as far away from your abode as possible, then arrange for some of your lackeys who did it to be caught by the barbarian so he can force them to reveal her whereabouts. Lackeys are cheap, you can always get more. (Then see paragraph II, Rule #4.)

6. If you were stupid enough to kidnap her, under no circumstances ever molest the barbarian's girlfriend in any way, shape or form — even to the extent of criticizing her make-up. If you do, you might as well go immediately and jump off the nearest tower, because the barbarian, who never gets laid, will be so pissed off your death will be a certainty.

7. When he arrives at a local village inn for food and lodging, under no circumstances allow your minions to laugh at the barbarian's table manners, his hair, or his clothes. If he was pissed off before, this will *really* chap his ass and you might as well kiss yours good-bye, not to mention your minions, who are, of course, all dead meat from the first smile they offer.

8. Never send a demon/sprite/sylph/witch/dryad or other supernatural being of the female persuasion to harry and destroy the barbarian. Your agent will invariably fall in love/lust with those brawny-thews and turn on you faster than a New York cabbie offered $50 extra to get to the airport on time.

9. While barbarians as a rule are seldom religious, they invariably have a patron deity whose name they will intone in moments of great stress. For some reason, even though they offer their patron spirits nothing but curses, barbarians are greatly beloved by these gods, who will almost always tip the scales a hair in their favor at precisely the wrong moment for your carefully-laid plans. Find out which god he likes, then begin making offerings/sacrifices well in advance to curry the god's favor. And be not parsimonious about it, either. Barbarian gods love the poor — but really hate a wealthy cheapskate. Pull out the stops.

10. Do not think to hire a barbarian of your own to defeat the one coming for you. Barbarians stick together and this will do

nothing but cost you money and double your trouble, as the hireling will quickly see the error of his ways and turn on you, at least as fast as the female demon you dispatched earlier.

The rule of thumb is this: If there is a barbarian with muscles, a sword and a girlfriend in town, put your plans on hold. You can always destroy the world next week. What's your hurry?

Steve Perry's Hungry Barbarian Shrimp Stir Fry

3-4 TABLESPOONS HOT PEPPER OIL (YOU CAN MAKE THIS YOURSELF BY PUTTING CANOLA OIL INTO A SMALL BOTTLE AND ADDING FLAKED RED PEPPER AND LETTING IT SOAK FOR A COUPLE OF HOURS, OR USE THE COMMERCIAL HOT SESAME WOK-OIL VARIETY.)

1 POUND MEDIUM-SIZED SHRIMP

1 SMALL GINGER ROOT

1/2 CUP CASHEWS

2 MEDIUM CHINESE EGGPLANTS

2 MEDIUM CARROTS

1 CUP RAW CABBAGE, GREEN OR RED

1 CUP SUGAR OR SNOW PEAS, ENDS TRIMMED

1/2 CUP MUNG BEAN SPROUTS

1 PACKAGE CHINESE NOODLES. FRESH ARE BETTER, BUT YOU CAN USE DRIED.

SOY SAUCE, BLACK PEPPER

You'll also need a large skillet or wok, a pot big enough to boil noodles, a colander, and two spatulas or wooden spoons. This is a quick dish, but also messy — you'll spatter your stove and self a bit, so an oven-hood ventilation fan is useful if you have one, as is an apron.

The trick to doing good stir fry is the timing. Once you start, it all goes very fast and you won't be able to step far away from the stove. All the ingredients should be ready *before* you crank the fire up, so the ginger should be grated or finely sliced — about a tablespoon is usually enough — the shrimp peeled, the vegetables peeled and sliced — and angle cuts are better. (It is not necessary to peel the eggplant, which looks kinda like a purple cucumber, but do take the ends off before you slice it with angle cuts.)

You should already have your second pot, with about 1-2 quarts of water, heating. Stir fry noodles cook very fast, so you want to wait until you are nearly finished with the vegetables before starting the noodles. Bring the water to a boil slowly.

Over a hot fire, in a large skillet or wok — you'll need a lid, later — heat the oil until it starts to smoke. Add the grated ginger, stir, and then add the cashews. When the ginger starts to crisp, add the shrimp. Stir and turn frequently. A pair of bamboo or wooden spatulas work best; do it like tossing a green salad. Don't overcook, no more than two minutes or until the shrimp have turned completely pink. Remove from heat, put the shrimp into a bowl or colander. Add another dab of oil to the skillet, return it to the stove, then add the carrots. Stir, cook for 1-2 minutes, then add the eggplant and cabbage. Continue to stir for another 1-2 minutes.

Put the shrimp back into the skillet, add 3-4 tablespoons of soy sauce — it'll hiss some — then add the sugar peas (or snow peas) and the bean sprouts. Stir and cover with a lid. Add more soy sauce to keep a bit of liquid in the skillet; from here on out, you're steaming instead of frying. Put the noodles into the water, stir. The water will probably stop boiling. Allow it to come back to a boil, then add one cup of cold water to the pot. When it starts to boil again, the noodles will be about done. Don't overcook them. Drain the noodles in a colander, then add them to the skillet. Sprinkle the noodles liberally with soy sauce (you don't need salt, this stuff is loaded with sodium), and pepper to taste. Stir for about 45 seconds. Remove from heat.

Serves 3-4 polite people, 2 barbarians.

You can use mushrooms or other vegetables if you like, potatoes, even sliced apples, just about anything, just remember to cook the harder ones like carrots first, then add the softer ones later. If you are a vegetarian, you use a bit more oil and try hard tofu with the water pressed out in place of the shrimp.

———————◆———————

Steve Perry is the author of many Conan novels. Recently, he has published The Trinity Vector, The Digital Effect, Spindoc, The Forever Drug, *the New York Times best-selling Star Wars novel,* Shadows of the Empire, *and a collaboration with Leonard Nimoy,* Target Earth. *He also has written the Matador series, Aliens novels, comic book scripts, and cartoons scripts. His movie novelization,* Men in Black, *appeared during the summer of 1997.*

A Gift From the Sea –
For Body and Soul

When we take the raw materials of the earth (or sea) and work with them — touch them, manipulate them, taste them, revel in their heady smell and glorious colors, and then through a bit of alchemy transform them into delicious creations — we do honor to the source from whence they sprang."
— *Judith B. Jones*, A Religious Art

WHEN AT THE OREGON BEACH, we were explorers, adventurers, my husband and I. Gifts from the sea that we discovered became treasures that delighted us. We loved looking for agates, sand dollars, glass floats from Japan and other treasures washed up from ocean tides, but the gifts that we sought and savored together, that nourished our bodies and souls, and that I remember best were the living gifts that were not only an adventure to collect but an adventure to prepare for the table, a gift for the palate.

Our calendar was marked with the low tides that occurred in daylight hours; on weekends since we still had work week obligations. It was at these times we headed for the rocks where we knew mussels lived, equipped with gloves and a screw driver. They didn't give themselves up to us easily. We scanned for those that stuck out, making them easier to pry loose, and those unencrusted with barnacles that would be easier to clean. We preferred mussels of medium size, three to four inches in length. When we returned to the cabin, we used pliers to pull their strong "beard" of coarse black hair that enabled them to cling to the rock. We forced off the stubborn barnacles with the screw driver.

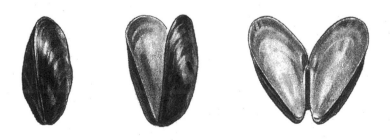

The meat from mussels is as tender as oysters, though with a soft firm texture, and as tasty as clams. My parents had used them only for bait for many years, fishing off the rocks along the coast, so they had trouble enjoying as food their soft orange flesh. To Dick and me they provided an extraordinary gastronomical delight and we enjoyed them steamed with wine, fresh oregano and Italian parsley from my herb garden, over linguini, or simply forced opened from the heat of the barbecue and served with a BBQ sauce.

I enjoy sharing these special meals of mussels with someone with whom I've have had the joy of gathering them. It's the recognition of the tie with God's creations in nature and the gratitude I feel for the gifts he has provided to feed the soul as well as the body; that makes this adventure a peak experience, from sea to table, meaningful and memorable.

Steamed Mussels in White Wine Sauce

4 CLOVES GARLIC, MINCED
1 CUP OLIVE OIL
1 BOTTLE DRY WHITE WINE
1 CUP CHOPPED ITALIAN PARSLEY
2 TABLESPOONS CHOPPED FRESH OREGANO
CRUSHED RED PEPPER TO TASTE
3 QUARTS MUSSELS

Sauté garlic in oil. Add remaining ingredients. Bring to a boil and reduce to one-half. Add mussels and stir to distribute sauce. Cook until mussels open, shaking pan frequently to cook evenly. Serves 10.

Jacque French has enjoyed writing for her satisfaction since retirement from teaching school in Beaverton, Oregon. She relishes a good book, and as librarian at Southminster Presbyterian Church, writes book reviews for the weekly church newsletter. She was inspired to write story-recipes when she participated in a food and theology class.

Rain Shorter Than
The Angle of Surrender

RAIN, SAYS BARTLETT'S, is a deluge showered, falls like cats and dogs, collects on roofs, dulls roots, comes early and later, falls on fringes, is hard and dirty, in Spain stays on the plain, is over and gone, makes not fresh again, monotonously falls, on corn a sad thing, wets the just and unjust, and something the earth soaks up unless you live in Portland's West Hills. One February I counted 17 slides on 3½-mile-round Fairmount, the latest street on which I live. I do not write many poems, but then I'd never seen my soul or rain run this way. Rain Shorter Than the Angle of Surrender, published in "Portland," magazine of University of Portland (Spring, 1996), paid $5. Brian Doyle is the sort of editor and writer we all need falling into our lives, any time of year.

Rain shorter than the angle of surrender
Unreasonable rain.
Goat-choking rain.
Rain soldering street to sky. Pigeon-toed, loping rain.
Rain standing by the side of the road.
Rain crazy enough to go ten rounds.
Righteous rain.
Rain in contempt of court.
Nevertheless rain.
Knee-bending rain.
Rain shorter than the angle of
surrender
Rain with meat on its bones.
Rain old enough to vote.
Perfect rain.
The rain right now.

Quick & Not-dirty Rainy-day Shrimp-Clam Chowder

3 16-OUNCE CANS NEW ENGLAND-STYLE CLAM CHOWDER
2 6½-OUNCE CANS CHOPPED CLAMS, WITH LIQUID
1 POUND FRESH OREGON SHRIMP (THE LITTLE ONES)

Heat on medium until barely bubbly, throw on oyster crackers (60 calories per 23 rounds), or dunk with a lusty bagel.

For all of 1997 and most of 1998, Sharon Wood worked on finishing her masters degree, updating The Portland Bridge Book *(scheduled to be reprinted in September 1998), and helping with grandchildren. When not discovering different ways to make money, Ms. Wood relates to Ed Wortman, her companion of five years who says he does not mind if she has less than 10 minutes to cook every year. Wood and Wortman are planning a fall wedding.*

I Need More Time to Write
Casserole

T HERE IS NEVER ENOUGH TIME both to make a living and
replace your living with writing fiction. Last time I was at the
Colony House with a group of writers, I was responsible for one
meal over the course of five days. I was in the grip of the muse and
pounding furiously on a novella, *Millennium in the City of Women*.
Everything that was not a word on the page was an annoyance.

O.K., What to cook? Fast. Filling. We're at the beach. Seafood.
Here it is:

Feeds as many people as the pan you use will feed.

FRESH SHRIMP
FRESH SCALLOPS
GARLIC AND/OR GARLIC SALT
BUTTER OR MARGARINE
TERIYAKI SAUCE
QUICK WHITE OR BROWN RICE
CREAM OF MUSHROOM (OR CREAM OF ANYTHING) SOUP
FRESH BROCCOLI
ANY OTHER FRESH VEGETABLES YOU THINK MIGHT TASTE GOOD

Preheat the oven to 350°F. Lightly grease the pan. I use a 9x9"
glass cake dish. Pour the shrimp and scallops into the dish so they
cover the bottom. I like a lot of scallops, so I put in a couple layers.
Pour in enough teriyaki sauce to douse all the seafood. Chop,
microwave for a couple minutes, and add the broccoli. Mix in
several tablespoons of butter. Sprinkle with minced garlic or garlic
salt. Cover in a layer of rice. Cover with cream of whatever soup.
Cover the dish with tinfoil and place in oven for 20 minutes.

Write for 20 minutes.

Stir the dish. Check the rice. If it is not absorbing enough liquid,
add a quarter can (cream of whatever) of water. Check the scallops
and shrimp. The dish is done when they are all white. You will
probably have to stir the dish several times while it is cooking to
cook all the scallops and shrimp without overcooking. Continue

cooking until the rice is tender and the seafood is cooked consistently without becoming dry and rubbery.

Set a nice table. Serve with wine, garlic bread and salad. Clean up, then go write some more.

———◆———

Eric Witchey is an Oregon Writers Colony board member who writes science fiction and fantasy. His agent is currently circulating his first novel, Echo, *among editors. Eric works in the Northwest computer industry as a technical writing consultant and teacher.*

Picking Bones

SHE LOVED TO COOK. She liked to watch eggs boil, the bubbles coming from underneath, sneaking out the top around the shell, the splash of the water as a perfect steam ring would puff up off the burner. She was delighted at the bright colors of vegetables which made a symphony of a salad.

When she picked the poached salmon meat off the bones, she focused down into the poaching pot, moved by the intricate webbing of fins, as the soft sweet orange flesh slid through her fingers into a bowl. No two bones were alike. Each had its own

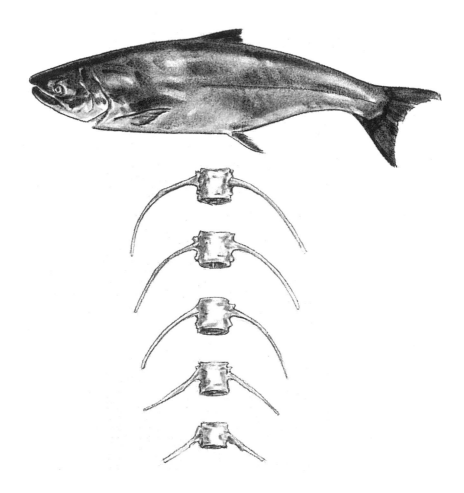

form and function. There were so many different lengths and shapes, curves and dents where they attached to the vertebra. They all created a fragile necklace of supple bone.

This fish had been caught in the Nehalem River. It was a fall Chinook that weighed in at 27 pounds. She was going to use the meat from the bones for a salmon salad.

"He put up a real good fight," her husband said. "It took me about twenty-five minutes to land him."

The two men, lounging in the living room launched into other stories about fish they had caught, comparing how hard he struck the line or struggled in the net.

"What did you do with *HER* eggs?" she hollered from the kitchen.

Following an uncomfortable silence, the discussion turned to curing eggs for steelhead season, and whether it's a good idea to use Hoochies or Slinkies on the Trask river.

"Thanks, old girl," she spoke to the bones in the pot. "Thanks."

Salmon Salad

½ POUND POACHED OR CANNED SALMON MEAT.
2 HARD BOILED EGGS
4 MINCED GREEN ONIONS
1 STALK CHOPPED CELERY
½ CUP MAYONNAISE
½ CUP YOGURT
1 TEASPOON DILL WEED

Combine above and serve on crisp greens or as a sandwich filling.

———————◆———————

Judith Massee is a prize winning poet and partner in Media Weavers publishing company. She currently writes the Poetry column for the Writers Northwest newspaper.

Clam Chowder

ISOBEL WORKED SWING shift, 5 p.m. to 2 a.m., at a data processing center. Before going to the office, she prepared supper for her husband, Art, leaving instructions.

She was taking a supper break at work when the phone rang. She answered it, and smiled. Art's voice warmed her. She liked talking to him. "Hey, you said in your note that you left clam chowder and to heat it on low."

She said, "Yes, that's right."

He cleared his throat. "I'm surprised. You never touch seafood. You always leave it for me to cook. What recipe do you use?"

She raised her eyebrow and rattled off the recipe from memory:

"Boil FOUR LARGE IRISH POTATOES and ONE HALF AN ONION with a FOURTH TEASPOON SALT and sprinkle with BLACK PEPPER. Chop up THREE SLICES BACON, fry until crisp, then drain. When the potatoes are tender, drain off the water. Cook a TABLESPOON OF WHITE CORNMEAL with enough WATER to make a paste, and stir into the potatoes. Add the bacon, a TABLESPOON OF BUTTER and a CUP OF CLAMS. Cover this with a CAN OF SCALDED EVAPORATED MILK mixed with an equal amount of WATER."

Art chuckled. "This tastes good, but it is chewy. I keep finding whole clam necks. How did you do them?"

Isobel stood up. "Oh, that's easy. I toss them in with a fork."

He was quiet a few seconds. "You didn't grind them?"

She gulped. "Grind them? Who, me?"

He laughed. "Well, just add the word 'GROUND' before clams in your recipe."

Isobel grinned. "I'm glad it tastes good. But if you want clams ground, guess who grinds them."

She hung up the phone and reached into her brown paper sack containing an apple, egg salad sandwich, and a recipe book. She settled down to look for something new to cook next for Art.

Isobel Tollefson chairs monthly readings for the Coos Bay Poet's Society and coordinated a poetry performance for the On Broadway Theater in Coos Bay, Oregon. She has contributed to The Beacon, the Southwestern Oregon Community College literary magazine, and In Our Own Voices, *the Oregon Writers Colony anthology.*

For Your Favorite Guy

THE WOMEN IN MY FAMILY have the tradition of fixing a special cake for the man they plan to marry. The chosen man isn't always aware of the significance of the cake, but it is an announcement to the women of the family of the potential bride's intentions. This family tradition has been around for seventy years.

My father is in his 90s now and my mother has been gone for 10 years. Yet, because his daughter, granddaughter and great granddaughter can bake this cake, his memories of his wife are revived each time this cake is served. Perhaps this recipe will become a tradition in your family, too.

Delicate Graham Cracker Cake

1/2 CUP SHORTENING
1/2 TEASPOON SALT
1 TEASPOON VANILLA
3/4 CUP SUGAR
2/3 CUP CHOPPED WALNUTS
2 EGGS, SEPARATED
2/3 CUP FLOUR
2 1/2 TEASPOON BAKING POWDER
1 1/3 CUPS OR 16 GRAHAM CRACKERS, ROLLED FINE
3/4 CUP MILK

Combine all except eggs, nuts and half the milk. Beat in mixer 2 minutes at medium speed. Add egg yolks and rest of milk. Beat 2 more minutes. Fold in beaten egg whites and nuts. Bake at 350°F for 30 minutes in buttered and floured 9x12" pan.

We serve this cake with strawberries and whipped cream for a topping.

Eva Jo Bess began writing in earnest two years ago and has been published 52 times between 1995 and 1997. She is as amazed as anyone at her good fortune at being published so often. But what also pleases her is that her husband of 40 years, her four children and her seven grandchildren all enjoy her cooking.

Chocolate Reflections

I GRAB A CAKE MIX from the shelf, dump it in a bowl, crack a couple of eggs on top, then add 2 glugs of cooking oil and 1⅓ cups water, measured with my rinsed out coffee cup. Switch on the mixer, and remember how I learned to bake during childhood summers in Mom's harvest kitchen. We used a cake recipe handed down from her mother, and Mom recited it to me by heart as I diligently followed every direction.

First the flour had to be sifted. I'd tear a piece of waxed paper to receive the powdery product, then scoop two heaping cups of flour from the big 100-pound bag. Carefully, I'd turn the knob of the sifter and a soft, white drift would heap into the center of the paper. Next, I'd spoon a measuring cup full of the white dust, careful not to pack it, level it off with a table knife and return it to the sifter. 2¼ cups of flour. After the flour was measured I added other dry ingredients: baking powder, salt, cocoa and sifted the mixture again onto the paper square, the drift now a faint auburn.

Then it was time for the technical stuff; three eggs, beaten until very thick. I'd break them into the mixer bowl, turn it on medium to whisk them up, then on high to thicken and turn them butter yellow. I'd measure 1⅓ cups sugar, then dribble it into the eggs, pushing the mixture away from the sides of the bowl with a rubber spatula, careful not to get it caught in the meshing beaters as the bowl spun and the mixture thickened. This process alone took about five minutes.

Grandma's chocolate cake was luscious, and what made it that way was 1⅓ cups rich cream instead of shortening. Mom poured it for me from a jar in the refrigerator, measuring ivory-colored cream so thick I'd have to lever it from the cup with a spatula.

Next, the dry ingredients stirred into the eggs and sugar *alternately* with the cream and vanilla, then let the reddish-brown batter spin and roll for several more minutes. Time enough to grease the pan. I didn't like to grease the pan, but I performed dutifully, trying hard to get the globs of shortening out of the corners and layering a thin, even film over the bottom and sides of the big cake pan, then dusting with cocoa. It was awhile before I learned to deftly turn the pan this way and that spreading the cocoa over the side and bottom of the oblong pan, then tapping it on the counter to collect the excess in one corner to be disposed of.

Mixer off, scrape the beaters, pour the batter into the pan, carefully scraping the bowl, then place it in the preheated oven that Mom always remembered to turn on to 350°F at the beginning of the project and I never did. Wait for 40 minutes. Time to lick the bowl and do the dishes, then I'd take a toothpick and push it into the center of that aromatic chocolate mound. When it came out clean, the cake was done, and Mom would take it from the oven and set it to cool before we made the fudge icing.

I discovered a lot of things while learning to make that cake. Long before fractions turned up in my math book at school I knew that $^2/_4 = ^1/_2$; I learned that if you keep the mixer on high and pour in dry ingredients what results makes you sneeze. I learned what *alternately* means, and that my mother has infinite patience and that the spinning beaters bend if you jam a spoon into them. The first time Mom said, "You make the cake today, I'm too busy to help" and I did everything by myself, I learned the joy of accomplishment when the hired men raved about the cake.

Today, I scrabble in the cupboard for the correct-sized pan. I settle on an 8" square, and a foil pie plate. A quick squirt of aerosol no-stick pan spray, then pour the batter into the pans and pop them in the oven I forgot to preheat. While checking the cake mix box for time and temperature, I realize this comparison is a metaphor for my life when I discover that each serving has 260 calories, and I should have used three eggs.

Sweet Cream Cake

3 EGGS — BEAT UNTIL VERY THICK
1¹/₃ — BEAT IN GRADUALLY CUPS SUGAR

Sift together:

2¹/₄ CUPS SIFTED FLOUR
3 TEASPOONS BAKING POWDER
1 TEASPOON SALT
¹/₄ CUP COCOA

Stir in alternately with dry ingredients:

1¹/₃ CUPS RICH CREAM (USE THE RICHEST AVAILABLE)
1¹/₂ TEASPOONS VANILLA

Beat until smooth. Pour into 9" layer pans or 13x9" oblong pan. Bake at 350°F: layers 25-30 minutes; oblong 40-45 minutes.

CHOCOLATE FROSTING

1 CUP(+) SUGAR
3-4 TABLESPOONS COCOA (TO TASTE)
1/2 CUP CREAM (TO THIN MIXTURE TO THE CONSISTENCY OF CREAM)

Cook over medium heat to boiling, stirring and watching so it doesn't scorch. Cook to softball stage; remove from heat. Add:

1 TEASPOON VANILLA
1 TEASPOON BUTTER

Beat until cool and it begins to harden before spreading on cake.

---

*Virginia Walters is a retired educator and freelance journalist. She grew up in the Palouse country of Eastern Washington where harvest was a busy time in the kitchen. She **does** retain most of the lessons learned in those days, and hopes she taught her daughter as well. She has lived in Alaska for many years, writing for a local weekly on assignment, and having poems and essays published locally and nationally in "little" magazines.*

Happiness Means Having a Pie Tin of Your Own

"YOU MUST DO WHAT PAPA SAID."

Hansena kept her back to her mother, rolling the pie dough quickly as her anger rose. "Why, Momma? Why?"

"Because he was your father and he knew what was best for you."

"He didn't know. He didn't know me, who I am or what I want." Hansena turned to face her mother. "I will not marry Karl."

"Karl is a good man and a good farmer. He will provide for you. You know your brother inherits the farm, and when he marries, there may not be a place for you here."

"What about you, Momma? Will there be a place for you?"

"Your brother has told me that I can live here as I always have."

"Isn't that generous of him!" Hansena's resentment flared. "Why should he get the farm and not you?"

"I can't work the farm."

"Maybe not, but at least you could own it and he could work for you instead of your being allowed to stay here because he says you can."

Hansena saw the despair etched in her mother's face.

"I have no choice, child. I have no place to go."

The two women stood in the kitchen. The heat from the cook stove gave them an excuse to brush their faces with their hands, to pretend they weren't brushing away tears.

"Momma, I'm going to find a place for us. Remember how Mr. Cockrell at the restaurant in town always wants me to bake pies and rolls for him? I'm going into town tomorrow to see him and maybe he will give me a job baking for him."

"You couldn't make enough to support the two of us, but you go and see if he can help you."

The next morning Hansena approached Mr. Cockrell in his restaurant and haltingly stated her need for a job. He thought her father's death was the reason for her being upset. As he attempted to put her at ease, she burst into tears and told him about her father's order that she should marry Karl and about her mother and the farm.

"Well, now, Hansena. I've known you since you were little." He hesitated slightly. "And I knew your father. He was not one to allow any view but his own. I can understand your wanting to make your own decisions now."

Hansena's face brightened as he continued. "If I can help, I will. I need baked goods for the restaurant. You can come here to work as a pastry chef. That sounds a little grand for this place, but you have a reputation for turning out good pastry and that will be a plus for the restaurant."

Mr. Cockrell paused. "Here's another idea. I own a small house over on Maple Street that's empty right now. You can live there if you like — rent free. That should help money-wise."

"Oh, thank you, Mr. Cockrell. Thank you. I'll work real hard. When can I start?"

"Next Monday will be just fine," her new employer replied. He chuckled as he enjoyed her eagerness.

Hansena could hardly wait to get home and tell her mother of her good fortune.

"What will folks think, you living in Mr. Cockrell's house?"

"Come live with me, Momma. Papa's dead. I know I sound like I didn't care about him, and I guess I really didn't. I was never able to please him and — oh, this is a terrible thing to say — it's a relief he's dead."

"Hansena, don't say things you will regret."

"Momma, I'm finally telling the truth. And I'm going to take my chances in town. Will you come?"

After a moment her mother straightened. "Yes, I will. But be sure you ask Mr. Cockrell if he agrees to my coming to live with you. We don't want to take advantage. I have a little money saved. You take it and use it."

"All right, Momma. I'm going to start packing now. May I take some of the pans from the kitchen? I've used them for so long. Remember the first pie I ever made? It was apple, and you taught me how to make a lattice top. I was so proud of it.

"Take what you like. I'll bring the rest when I come."

Hansena began working in the restaurant. Her reputation as a baker grew, and people would drive for miles to enjoy her pastries. "You should go into business for yourself. You'd make a fortune," the customers would say.

Mr. Cockrell began talking about financing a bakery for her. "Now, Hansena, this is strictly a business proposition, you understand. I expect to be paid back."

Again Hansena had good news for her mother. "My head's whirling, Momma. So much is happening so fast, but, oh, Momma, I know we can do it."

Here is a recipe you might be able to use.

Apple Creme Pie

1 CAN (20 OUNCE) SLICED PIE APPLES OR 3 CUPS FRESH APPLE SLICES
1 UNBAKED 9" PIE SHELL
1 CUP MARSHMALLOW CREME
1 TABLESPOON GRATED LEMON RIND
1 TEASPOON LEMON JUICE
1 CUP RAISINS
1/4 CUP FLOUR
2 TABLESPOONS BROWN SUGAR (PACKED)
1/4 TEASPOON CINNAMON
2 TABLESPOONS MARGARINE

Drain canned apples, reserving 1 tablespoon liquid. Arrange apples in pie shell. Combine marshmallow creme, lemon rind, lemon juice and reserved liquid. Mix with wire whisk until well blended. (If using fresh apples, substitute 1 tablespoon water for canned apple liquid.) Add raisins to marshmallow mixture. Mix well. Spread mixture over apples.

Combine flour, brown sugar and cinnamon. Cut in margarine until mixture resembles coarse crumbs. Sprinkle over marshmallow mixture. Bake at 375°F for 40 minutes.

———————

Elaine Estes was born in the Midwest, lived on the East Coast and now lives on the West Coast. Usually writes poetry. Has been published, including a chapbook.

Not by Bread Alone

M Y MOTHER, GRANDMOTHER and aunts were proud, proficient bread makers. They wore smudges of white flour on their faces and aprons after a baking session as their badge of accomplishment in domestic arts. The rich, succulent rolls they served at dinner proved their status as real cooks, accepted into the sacred circle of recipe exchange.

I, on the other hand, had never mastered the feel of just the right elasticity in the dough. It mixed too stiff or too limp, too sticky or too dry. It raised too much or not enough. It burned and stuck to the bread pan. I decided it wasn't worth the effort, bought bread at Safeway and felt my self-worth slump like another failed loaf. Mama and Grandma were too polite to discuss it in front of me.

Then I purchased a piece of modern technology that would boost my self esteem to the ionosphere: a bread machine. Excited to try my first loaf, I read the directions, measured flour, sugar, salt and yeast, added oil and water, took extra care to get the temperature of all the ingredients right on the money. Then I plugged in the machine and watched in astonishment as the little white box's lights glowed and the blade mixed, kneaded and rested the dough. In a couple of hours I could show off a perfect loaf of bread. Feeling exhilarated as I did learning to swim at age 40, I called Mama and invited her over for tea. "I have a surprise," I told her. "And," I added recklessly, "bring Grandma too."

Breathing the aroma of *my* bread baking, I hummed in happy anticipation. What a great feeling to reach one of those plateaus in life where you solve a tough problem and can move on. Perhaps I'd have the nerve to tackle those extra pounds I needed to lose.

Mama's car pulled up in front. I ushered her and Grandma in. "Look what I made," I said, leading them past the kitchen table where I'd set my best china teacups and a steaming pink flowered teapot. Ceremoniously, I flipped up the top of the bread machine and withdrew the baking pan. We all looked into its depths at a misshapen black lump.

"What is it?" asked Mama, clearly puzzled.

I couldn't get the darned thing to come out of the pan. It stuck to the Teflon interior like a peach to its pit.

Mama looked at Grandma and both shook their heads.

"Oh, it's all right, honey," said Grandma quickly, seeing my misery. "You can probably get along just fine on your looks. If you lose some weight."

Wheat Bread in the Machine

After trial and error, I made the following dense and heavy wheat loaf which Grandma and Mama liked. Add ingredients to your bread machine in the following order for a 2 pound loaf:

2 TEASPOONS ACTIVE DRY YEAST
2¹/₂ CUPS WHOLE WHEAT FLOUR
¹/₂ CUP RYE FLOUR
1 TEASPOON SALT
1 TABLESPOON CRACKED OR GROUND BLACK PEPPER
1 TABLESPOON MELTED BUTTER OR OIL
SCANT ¹/₂ CUP BROWN SUGAR
1¹/₄ CUPS LUKEWARM WATER
OPTIONAL: ¹/₃ CUP CHOPPED NUTS.

(Bread machines vary, so check instructions for proper time to add nuts or raisins.)

———◆———

Martha Miller, former executive director of The American Institute of Architects in Arizona, moved to the green hills of Portland three years ago. She spends her time writing short stories, endlessly revising a novel, and striving always to make a decent loaf of bread. She is president of Oregon Writers Colony.

Dreaming of Soup Stock

I WAKE AT DAWN, a dream slipping from my grasp. I lie there in the half-light, sure that the dream was important, wishing I could remember it. It's something about Ma, about the farmhouse in Maine where I grew up. Then memories from decades ago begin streaming back to me. I'm seven years old again, and Ma and I are in the farm kitchen, sitting at the big kitchen table. She is showing me how to pick all the remaining bits from a cooked chicken carcass. The carcass is on a white earthenware platter before us. Behind us on the black cast-iron stove, spiced sugar syrup in a pot bubbles and spits and sends a nutmeggy-cinnamony sweetness into the air around us. It is evening, and Pa, exhausted from the day's heavy farm labors, is asleep in his chair near the window, our marmalade-yellow cat draped around his shoulders.

"Look," Ma says, "see the chicken neck. It's curved, and the grain of the meat follows the curve. To get it off, bend the neck back against the curve."

I bend the neck. The flesh at the cut ends springs back away from the bones.

"Now just peel it off."

It comes easily away in my fingers. I eat the long bands of muscle.

"That's all you need to do with the neck," Ma says. "The flesh comes off quite cleanly. The back will take you longer. See those two ivory-colored rings? Those are the rims of hollows in the bone. Inside them is dark meat. You can dig it out with your thumb."

I dig. The thumb-sized pieces slip out whole. They are tender, rich and delicious.

"The smaller hollows over here are too small for thumbs. Pick up the back and use your front teeth. They'll fit into the depressions."

They do.

"Now turn the back over. See all the little pockets in the bone? The meat will come out of them the same way."

Beige, to ivory, to cream, to umber shapes of flesh in various sizes come out, each with its own taste and texture. Soon, only two larger dark masses are left, one on each side of the midline.

"What are those?" I ask.

"Just meat," she says. "Eat them, they're good."

They are.

When every bit of meat has been extracted, Ma smiles. "Now the bones are ready for the stock pot," she says.

Ma was a product of hard times, and my childhood, in the Great Depression of the 30s, was no exception. She taught me young the arts of survival. One of these was making soup stock. Her recipe took four days to complete, and started with the living bird.

Ma's Soup Stock

Day One: Kill the chicken. Dip in boiling water to loosen the feathers. Strip the feathers from the carcass and spread them out to dry in a safe place. They will be used later to stuff pillows. Eviscerate the chicken, but save the heart, liver and gizzard for the giblet gravy. Then stuff the bird with breadcrumbs mixed with chopped onion and diced sage leaves. Roast it along with carrots, onions and potatoes until they smell done. Make the giblet gravy, and start eating.

Days Two and Three: Eat the cold meat with hash made from the left-over vegetables.

Day Four: Strip the carcass of every bit of flesh and eat the bits as your reward. Fill a pot with cold water and add the chicken carcass. Throw in any vegetable tops, stalks and tough outside leaves you have. Though unchewable, these will yield a nourishing brew. Bring slowly to a boil and simmer for at least an hour. Allow to cool. Strain and chill the stock, and remove the layer of congealed fat on top. The finished stock is now a protein gel. Add fresh vegetables and cook until tender. Enjoy for two days at supper time with freshly made yeast rolls or corn muffins.

––––––––

Brenda Shaw grew up in rural Maine, attended Boston University, worked as a scientist in Scotland, and now lives in Eugene, Oregon. Her prose and poetry have appeared in periodicals and anthologies on both sides of the Atlantic. Her most recent publication is The Dark Well, *a book-length memoir of farm life during the Great Depression and World War II.*

For Peasants and Kings

IN MOST PLACES winter means those bleak and lonely months when roaring winds, snow and rain drown our summer dreams. Huddled indoors we retreat to the hearth, our kitchens. And if we are wise, we prepare the best of cold weather foods: soup. Because a kettle of homemade soup simmering on the back burner will banish the meanest case of winter blues.

Soup is sometimes maligned because in these pop-the-frozen-entree-into-the-microwave-times, many cooks haven't learned how to make the genuine thing. The stuff that heats you clear to your toes, clears your sinuses and warms a lonely heart.

Soup is misunderstood because it comes in so many forms; a meal for peasants and kings and folks in between. We associate soup with frugal cooks who throw the orphans of the refrigerator into a pot of water and end up with something the color of dirty dishwater. Or the thin gruel found in sick rooms. Admittedly soup makes a handy dinner for desperate times when an onion, potato, a few beans and a bone stretches to feed an entire family. But soup is also elegant, the sign of an accomplished cook. Yet for all its elegance, soup-making is easily learned; requiring a small dose of patience, an artful blend of ingredients, and heat to make it simmer.

True, some soups are best eaten under the blistering skies of summer. Served cold, these beauties have names that roll off the tongue like chocolate melting — vichyssoise, gazpacho. There are fruit soups made from melons and berries, dolled up with mint.

But real soup is cooked on a stove. After the leaves begin to fall. Real soup is hot and steams up the kitchen windows and reminds you of your grandmother. Real soup has character; chunky with vegetables, or pureed into a golden pudding. It's thick and true and makes us believe we will survive winter. With each comforting spoonful, no matter where we live, we're reminded of ice skating, sledding and caroling parties.

Sometimes soup is humble. Split pea. Country lentil. Navy bean. But despite its humble origins, soup deserves respect and good ingredients; vegetables chopped when they're crisp and bright skinned, not the shriveled onions, limp carrots and wilted parsley lurking in the shadows of the vegetable bin.

True, there are suspicious soups. Turtle, oxtail, boula-boula, sauerkraut. Ignore these monstrosities, they belong with bygone traditions like blackbird pie. Instead, make your childhood favorites. Chop and stir and grow calm. Size up your guests and choose between plain or exotic. Peanut. Lobster Bisque. Bouillabaisse. Sweet Potato.

Start with a big kettle, thick skinned and friendly. For a meat-based soup, cover the ham hock or chicken with water or stock. Add a chopped onion, celery, parsley, bay leaves and boil gently until the meat falls off the bone. Scoop it from the broth and set aside to cool. Later, pull the meat from the bone and toss it back in the pot. But first, skim off any fat. Now consider the bounty that comes next; peppers, potatoes, tomatoes, beans, rice, pasta.

For vegetarian soups start by sautéing minced pieces of the lily family — shallots, leeks and onion in olive oil. Consider adding garlic, peppers, celery. Sauté until all is wilted and golden turning to caramel and sweet. Now add more vegetables, bay leaves, herbs and stock.

Soup. Think hearty. Black bean. Borscht. Beef stew.

Suspect people who claim they can whip up real soup with a microwave, a few frozen packages, a can of this and that. Soup takes time. Soup must dance a slow boil.

Soup. Think surprises and deep flavors. Wine. Wild rice. Tarragon. Lemon grass. Sorrel. Mint leaves. Chestnuts. Ginger. Coconut milk. Raisins.

Soup. French onion. Carrot-leek. Avgolemono. Clam chowder.

Soup. There can never be enough. Mulligatawny. Minestrone. Cock-a-leekie. Zarzuela.

Soup. Don't forget toppings. Red onions, sour cream, grated cheddar, croutons, chives and cilantro.

Soup. Cream of tomato. Potato. Spinach. Broccoli. Cauliflower. In winter we must stay warm. We must make soup.

Sunday Night Seafood Stew

1 TABLESPOON SALT

1 TABLESPOON CORNMEAL

1 POUND LITTLENECK CLAMS, WELL RINSED

2 TABLESPOONS OLIVE OIL

1 LARGE ONION, DICED

1 SHALLOT, MINCED

3 CLOVES GARLIC, MINED FINE

1 GREEN PEPPER, DICED

1 YELLOW PEPPER, DICED

4 CARROTS, PEELED AND SLICED THIN

5 MEDIUM RED POTATOES, DICED

2 TEASPOONS DRIED BASIL

2 TEASPOONS SUGAR

1/2 CUP DRY RED WINE, SUCH AS CABERNET SAUVIGNON

28 OUNCE CAN STEWED TOMATOES

2 CUPS CHICKEN STOCK

1 POUND FIRM-FLESHED FISH (SUCH AS COD, HALIBUT, OR TURBOT) CUT INTO
    1-INCH PIECES

3/4 POUND MEDIUM SHRIMP, PEELED AND DEVEINED

1/2 POUND SCALLOPS

SALT AND PEPPER TO TASTE

Place the clams in a large bowl of cold water and sprinkle with cornmeal and salt. Let sit for one hour, rinse and drain. Heat the olive oil in a heavy soup pot, add onion and shallot, sauté about 5 minutes over medium heat. Stir in green pepper, yellow pepper, garlic, carrots, potatoes and basil. Cook for 5 minutes, then add sugar, stewed tomatoes, wine and chicken stock. Stir. Bring to a boil, then reduce heat, cover and simmer about 35-40 minutes until vegetables are tender. Taste and adjust seasonings (more basil may be added) Add fish, shrimp, clams and scallops. Cook about 8-10 minutes until clams are open. Serve with crusty bread or over hot rice. Serves 6-8.

Crab and Spinach Soup

2 RED PEPPERS, DICED FINE
3 MEDIUM SHALLOTS, MINCED FINED
$^1/_4$ CUP BUTTER
$^1/_4$ CUP FLOUR, SIFTED
1 POUND FRESH SPINACH, WASHED, DRIED AND STEMS REMOVED,
    CHOPPED INTO FINE SHREDS
12 OUNCES FRESH DUNGENESS CRABMEAT, FLAKED
4 CUPS CHICKEN STOCK
2 CUPS CLAM JUICE OR FISH STOCK
$^1/_4$ CUP SHERRY
$^1/_2$ TEASPOON NUTMEG
1 CUP WHIPPING CREAM
FRESH GROUND PEPPER TO TASTE

In a medium saucepan heat clam juice and chicken stock to a simmer. In a 4-quart soup kettle, melt 3 tablespoons butter over medium heat. Stir in shallots and red peppers. Sauté over medium-low heat until vegetables are soft about 6 minutes. Add remaining tablespoon of butter and flour, and stir constantly until flour is browned, 3-4 minutes. Whisk warmed stock into mixture, 1 cup at a time. Add spinach, nutmeg and sherry. Stir. Turn heat to medium and simmer 25 minutes. Whisk in whipped cream and crabmeat and season with pepper. Simmer 5 minutes until warmed through.

Hint: This soup is best when made one day ahead of time. To reheat, warm over low heat so that the cream doesn't curdle.

———

Jessica Page Morrell, former chef and caterer, is a full-time editor. She edits manuscripts, teaches writing classes and workshops in the Portland area, and has four published books about writing techniques. In the fall of 1998 Collectors Press will be publishing Writing Out the Storm, *with* Inspiration Notebook *to follow.*

Recipe for an Urban Legend

ALL —
This is a true story! I heard it from a friend of my mother's, who heard it from her cousin's husband's boss, who used to be married to the lady it actually happened to!

It seems this lady is eating dinner at the "Slug Shack" in West Eugene. She orders the most disgusting-sounding thing on the menu: stuff called Pink and Ugly Salad. It tastes kind of good, only in a weird sort of way. Now, this lady has eaten at lots of restaurants with lots of disgusting-sounding things since moving up from Roseburg, but this salad is weird enough she's sure it's been created by aliens.

Beets, pickles, completely unidentifiable crunchy things, all swimming in an opaque pink sauce. A delicate vinaigrette. Hint of dill. Something slimy, yet firm. She's never seen or tasted anything like it, anywhere! Even in Springfield. Immediately, she craves another serving.

She begs the chef to give her the recipe and is so persistent he finally agrees, though it's obvious he is nervous and afraid. He orders the bus boy to tattoo the ingredients and instructions on the lady's behind.

When she finally stops bleeding, her waiter, Al, hands her the bill. She sees that $20,000 (including gratuity) has been added to the total charges. She complains to the manager, who calls the chef from the kitchen to explain. The chef twirls his mustache and says something in a completely foreign language. That's when she knows that he's an alien. The manager suggests she pull down her pants so they can sort things out; when she complies, the chef points to her tattoo, smirks, looks upward to the heavens. "$20,000," he says in a voice unlike his own, "is what *anyone* who learns the secrets of the salad must pay!"

The manager apologizes, but there's really nothing he can do about the situation, as the chef is union.

The lady is furious. She refuses to be victimized, and devotes the rest of her life to seeking justice. For the first five years she shows her behind to everyone she meets. Her husband divorces her, goes to live with the Bagwan up in Central Oregon. She craves the salad on a near-daily basis, paints her car and the outside of her house pink. She plants rhododendrons and hangs fuschias. Alone with her halitosis, she has reached her darkest hour.

But things get better after copy machines are invented. She buys one for personal use and uses it days at a time. She hires an under-employed city councilor to post copies of the recipe on bulletin boards all over town warning others against ingesting it, even accidentally. She's invigorated by her renewed sense of purpose.

Things get sort of good — well, almost — once personal ads are invented. The lady sets up an account at the "Eugene Weekly" and leaves the recipe on her voice mail. She even meets a guy, but it turns out he's recently divorced, and not yet ready for a commitment.

Fast forward to the present day. Things are getting really great because the world wide web is invented. Now, communication and advice is only a phone call away. The lady designs a home page to warn the whole world about the secret salad, obsession, aliens, the greedy chef, and the skin disease she's been fighting that summer over the copy machine.

And that's where I find the recipe. Well, after I hear about it through channels, as I said. Please copy and forward to everyone you know.

Pink and Ugly Salad

3-4 TART APPLES, CHOPPED COARSELY
1 CAN CANNED BEETS, CHOPPED COARSELY
1¹/₂ CUP OF PICKLED HERRING WITH ONIONS
1 CUP SOUR CREAM PER CAN BEETS
1 CHOPPED DILL PICKLE PER CAN BEETS
VINEGAR FROM HERRING, 1 TEASPOON PER CAN

Marinate, but don't eat!

Serves billions, unless we stop it.

———◆———

Leslie What, a prolific author, teaches writing at Lane Community College in Eugene, Oregon, and has given workshops at OryCon and Breitenbush.

The Country Blue Door

I LIKED THAT back screen door. It was "Country Blue." The name and the color matched. Made of real wood, it pleased me. Probably just pine, but thankfully not metal or vinyl. And when painted, it came to life.

After I started recovering from a long-term illness, that's one of the first things I did. Went around painting the screen door and the outside trim. Sprucing it up. Getting it ready for life.

How I miss that door since we've moved. The sound of it. Like a soft clap in the forest. Noticeable, but a natural part of things.

And I miss the goings in and out. The red cedar deck we built. The birds we shared space with as they chirped and bathed, flapping their wings as if to scare away our cat.

Amazingly, we all shared the deck. Birds, friends, the cat, and two children plus two adults, so to speak. All with a kind of grace.

One summer day I painted on my canvas there alone with only classical music for company. As I worked, birds flocked into the cherry tree beside and above me. Soon they sang so enthusiastically that I felt as if we were all delighting in these divine moments of creation — together. A private concert of joy that no one else could hear. Made so much more because of the bird's sweet voices, so freely given.

Nothing else was necessary.

Another warm August day, I made a complex tasting, cold gazpacho soup, and had the courage to serve it to three teenage boys, Jimmy and Julian, and their friend Kevin. Outside, on the deck, I served it with style, then held my breath, as I knew it competed with the fast foods teens loved. After the first tentative sip, they gulped it down and, shock of all shocks, asked for more!

Definitely one of my greatest accomplishments!

And on a spring day, a turning point: Allen and I on the deck. I have a picture of it in my mind. It's as if I look outside through the large dining room window and see us both there.

Allen, asking me to marry him. A quiet, intense time. The joy of both of us as I said "Yes." And then a hug — a long one — that I still carry with me today.

It was a good deck. A good door. A door that opened up to a place the birds thought was a sanctuary. The blue door reminds me — so did we. All of us did a lot of singing there.

I had visited Spain and learned to love gazpacho soup on hot summer days. Finally, I came up with a recipe that pleases my memories and my family. Prepare it ahead, in the cool of the morning, for a real treat for the cook.

— from Sheila's book in progress about writing life stories

Gazpacho

4 RIPE TOMATOES
1 CUCUMBER
1 GREEN PEPPER
2 CLOVES GARLIC
1 ONION
^{1}/$_4$ CUP APPLE CIDER VINEGAR
1 TABLESPOON LEMON JUICE
^{1}/$_4$ TEASPOON PARSLEY (^{1}/$_2$ TEASPOON FRESH)
^{1}/$_4$ TEASPOON TARRAGON (^{1}/$_2$ TEASPOON FRESH)
^{1}/$_4$ TEASPOON OREGANO (^{1}/$_2$ TEASPOON FRESH)
^{1}/$_2$ TABLESPOON GARLIC POWDER
^{1}/$_8$ TEASPOON CAYENNE (TO YOUR TASTE)
1 CUP WATER OR TOMATO JUICE

Coarsely chop tomatoes, cucumber, green pepper, garlic and onion. Puree in blender, along with the vinegar and lemon juice. Pour into bowl. Chop and add: parsley, tarragon, Italian oregano, along with garlic powder and cayenne pepper. Mix in approximately 1 cup water (or tomato juice), to desired consistency. Then stir and chill well. Garnish with cucumber or lemon slices, if desired. Serve with toasty garlic bread and enjoy!

In the summer, I like to grow and use fresh herbs. Just rinse, pat dry and chop, removing any stems. Softly pound on them after chopping to release their full flavor. Fresh tomatoes and herbs give this recipe the chef's touch, even pleasing teenagers.

———◆———

An inspirational, how-to writer, Sheila Stephens guides people through a transformative process, whether it's in her book, Light Up Your Dreams with Love *(under consideration for publishing), or her writing classes.*

Not for the Chicken-Hearted
or
The Butcher Most Fowl

THE KOREAN BUTCHER, dapper in his starched white apron and white gloves, bowed in greeting, "Hi! Bif?"

"Hi! No beef. Chicken!" After one week in Seoul and seven pounds of ground beef (due to a communication glitch on my first butcher visit) my husband Paul and I were looking forward to a nice chicken dinner.

"No chick!" The butcher tapped the cow-shaped wooden meat map on the wall. "Bif!"

"Where is chicken?"

He crinkled his nose in disgust and pointed down the hill.

I set off, fascinated by the little shops crowding the lane, with their colorful awnings, ancient red tile roofs, and windows displaying everything from toys and coal tongs to bras and garlic. Merchandise spilled out the doorways onto the asphalt — burlap bags of peanuts, crates of apples and onions, buckets of bamboo-handled toilet brushes. The freezer outside the grocery was packed with popsicles. The fishmonger's table aired white-eyed fish and glistening squid. But in all this abundance I hadn't glimpsed a single chicken.

I stopped before the one shop on the block I hadn't peeked into this week, put off by its window painted all over with neon-green Korean letters, and the hulking black Harley parked in front. But maybe those letters spelled "GET YOUR CHICKEN HERE!"

I pressed my nose to the glass door. Eureka! Right behind the window was a display case stuffed with plucked chickens.

I slid the door aside and stepped in, engulfed by the throat-closing stench of chicken guts. Sunlight filtered through the letters on the window, tinting everything green — the concrete walls, concrete floor sloping to a center drain, utility sink, tree stump chopping block, and curls of polka-dotted fly paper twitching above the case of green-tinted chickens.

Flies buzzed.

No butcher in evidence. Relieved, I began to back out — then stopped, remembering Paul's dear face, so hopeful for chicken.

In the shadows at the back of the shop I spied a wall made of paper and wood with a Japanese-style sliding panel. I called out, "*Yoposayo?*" Greetings. The only Korean word I knew. No answer. I stepped past the display case. "*Yoposayo!*"

The panel scraped open six inches, revealing a man's head lying on the floor, glaring at me. The panel banged shut. I heard a loud sigh, rustling sounds, then the panel opened all the way. A paunchy man in T-shirt, black leather jacket and polyester slacks stood in his stocking feet, rubbing his eyes. A purple satin comforter lay rumpled on the yellow linoleum floor. Next to it a TV flickered soundlessly.

I smiled apologetically for waking him and pointed to the case of chickens. He scratched his neck, slipped his feet into pink plastic slippers and shuffled past me toward the case, stopped, turned his back to me, and unzipped his pants. I jumped back as a steaming golden stream hit the floor drain. The smell of urine mixed with gutted chickens. The buzzing splash harmonized with the flies. I stood transfixed, wondering — was I being insulted, or was this the cultural norm for chicken butchers? Should I walk out in a huff — or buy Paul his chicken?

The butcher zipped up, reached bare-handed into the case, snatched up a chicken by its headless neck and whomped it onto the chopping block. Its feet dangled over the edge. He grabbed a cleaver from the sink, frowned at me with a questioning eyebrow and mimed a hacking motion over the scrawny carcass. I felt myself nodding "Yes." Quartered would be good.

The cleaver flashed and crunched and before I could yelp "*Yoposayo!*" he'd hacked the bird into bite-sized bits.

He tossed the cleaver into the sink, stuffed the bits into a baggie and flicked the feet into a wicker basket overflowing with yellow chicken feet.

He grunted something. I tore my gaze from the wicker basket. He held up four fingers.

"What?"

He scowled and came down in price to three fingers.

I dug three bills from my purse and traded them for the oozing bag. He ambled back to his room, stuffing the bills into his back pocket with slimy fingers.

Safe outside I took several deep cleansing breaths, letting the bag drip at arms length, and resolved that next time Paul could buy his own chicken. I'd stick to bif. I set off for home, eager to tell him my adventure. *After* dinner.

What Paul ate —

Korean Chicken Surprise

1 CHICKEN, IN PIECES
1 GARLIC CLOVE, MINCED
1 ONION, CHOPPED
2 APPLES, PEELED AND SLICED INTO EIGHTHS
A HANDFUL OF PEANUTS
1 CAN APPLE JUICE CONCENTRATE, UNDILUTED
SALT AND PEPPER TO TASTE

Sterilize chicken by sautéing with garlic and onion. Drain. Add apples, peanuts, apple juice. Simmer until apples tender. Add salt and pepper. Feel free to improvise. I recommend deboning the chicken before hacking it to bits.

———◆———

C. Lill Ahrens: cartoonist and illustrator since 1972. Wife, mother, and, since 1989, a full-time writer. Belongs to four critique groups: two weeklies, one monthly, and one emergency.

Gruîtt: A Christmas Eve Tradition

GRUÎTT — THE WORD STARTS with a growl and ends with a tongue thrust — sounding hearty and toothsome. My Norwegian great-grandmother, Laura Frostad, made the dish to please my Swedish great-grandfather, Per Eric Johnson. Gruîtt, then, is a Swedish rice entree, cooked with love to warm one's insides on blustery, snowy evenings.

I say "snowy," for from shivery Scandinavia my great-grandparents emigrated to America to settle in a similar Nordic environment — St. Paul, Minnesota.

My grandfather, Henry Eugene, was the youngest of their nine children, five of whom died before the age of six. Minnesota winters in the late 1880s were harsh.

By the time Henry married Gertrude McLaughlin, cooking gruîtt had become a holiday tradition. Laura boiled the rice all day long, then served it as the *pièce de résistance* for Christmas Eve dinner. She accompanied the meal with lutefisk, flatbread and a variety of butter cookies.

Though of Irish descent, my grandmother Gertrude chose to carry on the tradition for her children, "Hank" Jr. (my father) and Marilouise. Gertrude, however, disliked lutefisk, so she dropped that from the menu, offering instead cold cuts of turkey and ham.

My father wed Grace Knight and had five children (I'm the oldest); Marilouise married and produced six offspring. We 11 hungry grandchildren determined what else was served for Christmas Eve dinner — gruîtt just wasn't enough. Our holiday buffet table became filled with more "child-friendly," albeit less ethnic selections — platters of Monterey jack and American cheese, rye and wheat bread, crackers, cheeseballs, jello and Waldorf salads, fruitcake and nuts.

Gruîtt is the only "foreign" food to make the cut for the present Johnson generation. As of Christmas 1996, "Nana" Gertrude, 91 years old, still managed to cook the rice for her grandchildren and great-grandchildren.

Another tradition that has survived since Laura's time is adding an almond to the gruîtt, along with the announcement, "Whoever finds the nut in their bowl wins a prize." In the 1960s the victor received a dollar — big money for us youngsters!

Now in the '90s, the ante has been upped to five dollars. This year my sister-in-law Lisa, eight months pregnant with Baby Boy Johnson (Nana's 22nd great-grandchild), took home the booty (for booties?).

Despite the almond inducement, what most impressed me about gruîtt was watching my grandmother stir the snow-white mixture as it slowly boiled in an enamel pan atop the stove. She'd run and check the rice every fifteen minutes like a worried mother who inspects her baby while it naps. Grandma wanted the gruîtt, when finished, to melt in the mouth, softened yet still firm (*al dente*, the Italians say), and creamy like a rich custard.

Gruîtt

2 POUNDS WHITE RICE
6 QUARTS MILK
3 QUARTS WATER
PINCH OF SUGAR AND SALT

Pour rice and 2 quarts water into a large oval pan. Set this pan within a roaster pan which is filled with a small amount of water. Place the pans atop a stainless steel rack arranged so that the pans sit above two stove heating elements. During the cooking process, always add enough water in the roaster pan so that the liquid never boils away.

Cook at medium heat for 5-6 hours, stirring the rice in the oval pan until its 2-quarts' water evaporates. Continue adding the last quart of water and the 6 quarts of milk, stirring periodically to prevent sticking. Just before done, add a pinch of sugar and salt to bring out the flavor.

Serve in bowls with half 'n' half or milk, along with toppings of sugar, cinnamon and a pat of butter. Makes about 20 bowls.

Linda Leslie is a Portland freelance writer who has published in various periodicals, including Writers Northwest, El Mundo de Oregon and Higher and Higher magazine. In 1995 she was named a Fishtrap fellow in fiction. She writes for the Willamette Writer and serves on the boards of that organization and Oregon Writers Colony. She is rewriting a historical novel, Dolores, *about a woman who participated in the Mexican Revolution of 1910.*

Memories of Lutfisk

IS ANY FOOD MORE MALIGNED than lutfisk? Does anyone wax poetic over its heavenly aroma, terrific texture, or appetizing color?

Never!

The secret of that enigmatic Scandinavian soul food remains a mystery. Served with pride every Christmas, lutfisk has been a tradition for Swedes and Norwegians across their adopted land. If you were invited to Christmas Eve dinner, it was there. You were welcome to try it, but no one urged you. As my mother said, "If you don't eat it, that's fine — so much more for me!" There was always plenty of other good Christmas food on the table. No one goes hungry at a Scandinavian dinner.

I'm not sure how the tradition started. Maybe it was in Norway (where they spelled it with an "e" . . . lutefisk.) My great-aunt by marriage, Martha Olson, told us about the codfish caught by fisherman off the coast of Norway. It was dried and stacked like cord-wood in an outdoor storeroom for daily meals all winter. It wasn't a holiday food; it was a staple. However, when the Norwegians immigrated to this country they could get it only rarely. Then it became a treat for special occasions.

Maybe the Swedes imported the fish and the tradition from Norway. My mother wrote about her father's store in Sweden which included a meat shop where he sold my grandmother's sausages and, at Christmas, lutfisk. Mother learned from him how to prepare the fish. Many years later she described the process in the cookbook that she edited for our Lutheran church in Butte, Montana, a book I still use.

This is the process that I remember as a child, especially the part about my father sawing the dried cod, which looked to me like old boards, into smaller pieces. Here is the recipe, as mother published it:

Lutfisk (16 big servings)

Time required, 12 days

4 *POUNDS OF GOOD DRIED COD*
1 *HEAPING TABLESPOON LYE*
3 *GALLON CROCK OR JAR*

Saw fish in 6-inch pieces and soak until skin pulls off fairly easily, changing water every day for 5 or 6 days. Remove skin and bones and waste. Dissolve lye in about a quart of hot water in a three-gallon crock or glass jar. Fill crock half full with cold water, mixing lye thoroughly with water. Place fish pieces in this solution, adding enough water to fill crock. Stir enough to mix brine well. Cover and let stand in cool place for 3 days, changing water daily or oftener. (If some pieces are much thicker than others, they may be left in lye a day longer.) When boiling the fish, drop pieces into very salty boiling water, and keep at boiling point until done, about 15 minutes. Do not allow to boil hard. Serve with melted butter or cream sauce.

CREAM SAUCE FOR LUTFISK (1 pint)

Melt ½ *CUBE BUTTER* in sauce pan. Stir in ¼ *CUP FLOUR*. Mix well. Add gradually *1 CUP MILK* and *1 CUP HOT LUTFISK BROTH*. Cook slowly, stirring occasionally. (If sauce becomes lumpy remove from fire and beat until smooth.) Flavor with *SALT AND WHITE PEPPER* to taste. For richer sauce, add more *BUTTER*. Thin with milk if necessary.

— *Mrs. John Pearson*

On Christmas Eve my mother served a generous and festive meal. There was korv (potato sausage), kalv sylta (jelled veal loaf), bruna böner (sweet-and-sour brown beans), a jelled salmon mold, boiled potatoes, and, of course, lutfisk with your choice of melted butter or cream sauce. We were told that the melted butter was at Auntie's request, because that is the way the Norwegians served it. The warm fragrance of korv and sweet-and-sour beans nicely masked the smell of the lutfisk in my memory of Christmas at home. Unfortunately my mother-in-law, on her first visit to my parents' home for the holidays, walked into the kitchen just as the steaming lutfisk water was drained into the cold kitchen sink. I don't think she even tried it after that aromatic introduction.

Our guests always included Auntie and Uncle and family friends Emma and Joe and Pete. Emma and Joe were comfortably round people who enjoyed a good meal. Lutfisk was a favorite! Besides, it was great fun to tease my brother and me with it. Santa Claus, in our home, came on Christmas Eve like the Swedish "jul tomte", and he wouldn't come until dinner was over. Emma, with a twinkle in her eye, would look at my little brother and say, "I t'ink I'll yust have some more lutfisk." Then there would be a sad sigh at having to wait even longer to open presents! When we weren't looking my father would steal away from the company. There would be a bang at the door to the living room. When we opened it we discovered that Santa had been there!

There are many ways to prepare and serve lutfisk ... (or lutefisk.) My friend Osie, a German turned Norwegian when she married, makes lefse, large Norwegian potato pancakes as big as dinner plates. The lefse are buttered and heaped with mashed potatoes and lutefisk. Melted butter or cream sauce (made with mustard) is poured over all, and the lefse are folded up to eat like tacos. It's a heavy meal, and they love it. Some people bake lutfisk, and I've heard of a lutfisk casserole.

Today lutfisk can be purchased at some meat markets around the holidays. It is already prepared for the final boiled meal . . . no sawing up dried cod and changing the lye water! For Scandinavians who treasure the memory of Christmas dinners, it is even worth polishing silver tarnished by the fish. You might say that lutfisk is a strong favorite!

———◆———

Betty Pearson McCauley was born in Butte, Montana, to immigrant parents, where her family celebrated their Swedish heritage at the table, particularly at Christmas. She now tries to find time to write while enjoying four grandchildren, pursuing volunteer commitments and fitting in the good things in life — folk dancing, bird watching, church, music, reading and good friends.

A Tzimmes at the Rosenbergs

ENOUGH OF ATOMIC SPIES!" Ruth Robinson switched off the radio. "Can you keep a secret? Did you know my father is a distant cousin of Julius Rosenberg?"

"No kidding!" Molly Gladstone's mouth dropped open.

"We changed our name." Ruth shrugged. "Like names ending in -stone used to end in -stein."

"Yeah." Molly nodded.

"By the way, want to stay for dinner?"

Molly grinned her acceptance. Intellectual conversation with Ruth's parents beat listening to her own parents settle fights between her sisters and brothers. The girls, Molly tall and gawky,

Ruth short and rounded, descended a wide carpeted staircase to the dining room.

Ruth's father dominated the head of the mahogany table. He motioned the girls to sit down with a broad sweep of his hand. "And what have you been discussing today, my dears?"

"The Rosenberg case, Daddy," Ruth said.

"There really isn't any case against them," Molly broke in. "They couldn't have done what they are accused of."

Ruth's mother came bustling in with a spicy smelling casserole. A tiny bird of a woman, she hovered over everyone at the table in turn. "Such a tragedy, the parents of two young children. Tzimmes, Molly dear?"

Molly heard only a mumble of consonants, but she held out her plate for what looked like Irish stew.

Ruth received only half as much as Molly. "Zaftig's not so becoming for a young girl," said Ruth's father. His hands outlined voluptuous curves in the air.

Ruth folded her arms across her chest and changed the subject back to the Rosenbergs. "It's because of anti-Semitism . . . ."

"It's part of McCarthyism, to scare the left," said Ruth's mother.

Molly took a bite of the tzimmes. Sweet and savory flavors complemented each other. She swallowed and pointed out what she thought was the key factor in the case. "The Russians knew the only real secret, the chain reaction of U^{235}, before the war."

Ruth's father smiled. "My daughter doesn't bring home many friends, but when she does, it's a smart girl."

Ruth's mother said, "And she helps our Ruth with her homework."

Molly beamed.

Ruth slumped down in her chair. "They were convicted because they were Jews."

Molly said, "You couldn't put the secret of the atomic bomb on a few scraps of paper, any more than you could the secret of the internal combustion engine."

Ruth pushed her small portion around her plate. "Jews have been scapegoats throughout history."

"More tzimmes?" Ruth's mother passed the casserole to Molly. "Just a glass of milk, please."

The clink of silverware against china ceased. "We don't have any; we keep kosher in our family," Ruth said.

"Kosher?" asked Molly. "What's that?"

Ruth stood up. "You're not really so smart, you're always show-ing off, and you're not even Jewish," she wailed. She flung her napkin to the table and rushed from the room, stifling a sob.

"Ruth, don't make a tzimmes, it doesn't matter whether Molly is Jewish," Ruth's mother said.

Ruth's father turned to Molly. "Everyone is welcome in our home."

Tzimmes

¹/₂-1 POUND STEW BEEF
¹/₄ CUP MATZO MEAL
1 TEASPOON GARLIC SALT
1 TEASPOON BLACK PEPPER
4 TABLESPOONS COOKING OIL
2 CLOVES GARLIC
2 NICKEL SIZE SLICES GINGER
1 ONION
8 CARROTS

2 YAMS
2 WHITE POTATOES
24 PITTED PRUNES
1 STICK CINNAMON
2 CUPS ORANGE JUICE
¹/₄ CUP HONEY
¹/₄ CUP BROWN SUGAR
1 TABLESPOON SOY SAUCE
WATER

Cut beef into 1" chunks. Dredge in matzo meal seasoned with garlic salt and black pepper. Brown in oil in Dutch oven.

Chop the garlic, ginger, and onion, cook in oil till onion is clear. Peel and cut the other vegetables into chunks. Add carrots first, then yams, then white potatoes. Add prunes and cinnamon. Pour orange juice, honey, brown sugar, and soy sauce over mixture. Add enough water to fill Dutch oven.

Cover, bake at 375°F about 1¹/₂ hours until carrots are soft.

For vegetarian version, omit beef and cooking oil, substitute butter.

————————◆————————

When Sheila Smith (b. 1939) is not writing, she walks dogs. Training dogs to heel is like writing fiction. "Show, don't tell."

Non's Legacy

MY MOTHER, Rose Benton, (we called her Nonnie), was that just-about-rarest-of-all-creatures — a woman of great beauty who paid little heed to it. Though always well-groomed and nicely dressed, she was never vain about her looks.

But her *cooking*? That was another story!

Yet, "vain" is not the proper word; it implies excessive pride. Her culinary gifts — ethnic (Jewish) or "generic," *warranted* pride and *no* amount would've been excessive!

Family was her loving focus, but Cooking was her passion. The recipes she clipped from publications of every description overflowed recipe boxes, books and notebooks. Favorites were taped to kitchen cabinets and stashed in several places throughout the apartment she and my dad lived in. (Long after Alzheimer's disease robbed her of the ability to cook, she still clipped recipes.)

Everything she prepared not only tasted good, it looked glorious too. Her Thanksgiving dinners were artful labors of love with everything made from scratch; each platter presented beautifully on a table whose cornucopia centerpiece overflowed with a bountiful harvest of squash, nuts, fruit and autumn leaves she saved and dried for the occasion.

One of her cakes earned her an Oregon quarter-finalist prize in the Pillsbury Bake-Off. Others she adorned with amazingly realistic "gardenias" painstakingly hand-fashioned from marshmallows and completed with real leaves.

Her grandson's first birthday cake was a miniature carousel complete with horses, and as he and his sisters grew up and attended college, she sent them mouthwatering care packages I suspect sustained them as much or more than the "financial packages" we supplied.

Every party we ever had, she made special with her exquisite, mouthwatering contributions. And, speaking of contributions, throughout the first year of our marriage, my new husband and I were kept "afloat" by Friday night dinners with my folks and the left overs and "send-overs" she supplied while I learned to cook. (No, she never taught me how when I was growing up. I wasn't particularly keen on cooking — only eating! — and she wasn't enamored of company in the kitchen while she worked, not even me.)

Now, when I think of the marvelous variety of foods she made, what comes to mind first is neither very unusual nor particularly ethnic — just a homely, life-sustaining, magnificent-tasting lima bean and barley soup, guaranteed to get you through the coldest winter night warmed, nourished, and restored.

As this is written, my mother is still alive, her face still beautiful. But her talents — her joy — her reality — all, have been extinguished by Alzheimer's disease.

How deeply I wish she could know that nothing material could *ever* mean as much as her unique legacy; a wealth of heartwarming memories of the unforgettably delicious, wonderful meals our beautiful Non flavored with her selfless love for us all.

Non's Lima Bean and Barley Soup

2 CUPS LARGE LIMA BEANS, RINSED (DON'T USE BABY LIMAS, NOT
*   AS FLAVORFUL)*
1¹/₂ POUNDS BEEF CHUCK FOR SOUP (ARM CHUCK IS BEST IF YOU CAN FIND IT)
1 MEDIUM ONION, CHOPPED
2-3 CARROTS, CHOPPED
2-3 STALKS CELERY, CHOPPED
6-8 WHOLE ALLSPICE KERNELS
²/₃ CUP PEARL BARLEY, RINSED
1 BAY LEAF
SALT/PEPPER TO TASTE (USE WHOLE PEPPERCORNS, 6-8, BEST)
COLD WATER, 3-4 QUARTS (TO COVER MEAT, AND THEN SOME)

Bring beef only to a boil; skim scum. Reduce heat and boil gently, covered, at least one hour. Bring to rolling boil again; add rinsed barley while soup is boiling hard. Reduce heat to medium boil and cook another half hour or so.

Add all remaining ingredients; cook at least two more hours, or until meat is tender and soup is tasty. Stir frequently; it loves to stick to the pot bottom.

Note: After overnight refrigeration, a spoon will stand upright in it. To thin, don't use straight water but a mix of about ³/₄ water to ¹/₄ beef bouillon. Don't overdo the bouillon; it overpowers the soup's distinctive flavor. — *Rose Rebecca Benton, circa 1930s*

Jewish Cooking

When I got married and started to cook
  I figured there would be a book

Detailing how to make a "blintz"
  The way they did it back in Minsk

Alas! I learned to my dismay
  That I would never see the day

A book could translate, "just a pinch"
  Into a real, lead-pipe cinch . . .

A never-fail recipe
  For second generation me.

So, I am happy and content
  With Friday nights and heaven sent

Mamas who rescue those like me . . .
  . . . from package-mix monotony.

Julie Benton Siegel attended UCLA, majoring in fashion design/psychology which she says equipped her to design Freudian slips. She began writing primarily humor and light verse in her early 30s. She lives in Oregon with her husband and has three children and a granddaughter.

Rare Hungarian Delicacies

M Y MOTHER WAS SUCH A WONDERFUL COOK that I became very good at doing dishes. Still, I'd have been at sea in my own first kitchen if it hadn't been for a house rented with four other grad students and teachers.

It was a wonderful household, despite our varied interests (a physical therapist, a student teacher, a musician, an "experienced" second grade teacher, and a poet). We each threw $5 into the kitty each week. Each cooked dinner one night a week; on weekends we collaborated. I had drawn Friday night, being new to the group, and would find the food purse nearly empty but the refrigerator nearly full — with leftovers from Adele's shrimp casserole, Dottie's "economical" steaks (from the horse-meat market), Margo's healthy liver and onions, and Jo's quick as a wink spaghetti or lasagna. A small container of those sauteed carrots, half an onion, two dead-ripe avocados — and a student budget — and if you threw it all in one pot it would be . . . ghastly.

So how I learned to cook was opportunistically. Recipes were useless. Sniff this, inhale that. What might combine pleasantly? What new addition would bring reincarnation to the tired stew? I knew I was learning when my pals began inviting their beaux to dinner on Friday nights! (Guests threw fifty cents into the kitty, and the more affluent ones might bring a bottle of wine.)

So in my first kitchen, I cooked for my student-teacher husband with the courage of an eager novice and an unfettered imagination. There was no celery in the house? Ah, but I had a can of water chestnuts that I bought on sale. The recipe called for *that*, but *this* was all I had around. *These* things would be compatible in a soup, but *those* had better be the grace-notes in a salad.

But there was always the hungry end of the month, regular as turning the calendar page. Purse is empty, refrigerator nearly so.

Oh lordy, I didn't thaw the hamburger when I dashed off to teach school this morning. Well, that bacon fat I saved from breakfast will zing it up a little, if I throw the frozen brick in the fry pan, brown one face of the brick, flip it over and scrape the 'done' part off, flip it again, and scrape off the other browned side, until it was all nice brown crumbles. A little salt and pepper now. In between flips I'd diced the big onion that was hanging around. And what about the tomatoes I'd canned? Throw in the whole jarful, once the onions had been stirred into the meat for a few moments. Ah yes, there was a little zucchini that hadn't made it into the green dish yesterday. Hey, half a green pepper!

Smelling pretty good, but not really super. With all that tomato, how about some oregano, marjoram, garlic? Go Italian.

Hmm, pretty soupy. Well, there's quick brown rice - that would give it all some coherence.

"Wow," said Alan, whose mother cooked recipes with fancy names. "What have we tonight?"

I knew he liked names. I knew he felt more secure when he thought I knew what I was doing. "A Rare Hungarian," I said breezily.

"That's what it's called?"

I nodded, my mouth full. It WAS good.

"It's a delicacy! You could serve this in any fancy restaurant."

I didn't tell him it was "rare" because I'd never again have exactly the same leftovers, and it was Hungarian because it was the hungry end of the month. "Okay," I said. "It's a Rare Hungarian Delicacy".

But one month I didn't have any tomatoes left. While the meat was browning, I searched the pantry. Hey, a can of mushroom soup, and there were some mushrooms in the refrigerator. Lots of onions this time, and some celery. Go basil and dill, perhaps, and quick white rice.

"What's THIS?"

"A Rare Hungarian."

"It is NOT what you made last time."

So I had to confess. Rare meant "held over for one more day, due to popular demand," and "Hungarian" meant— "it's the 30th and we don't get paid till Monday."

We had red Hungarians and pale Hungarians, and, in a fit of frenzied panic, a Hawaiian Hungarian with half a can of pineapple and some Canadian bacon. Alan stopped asking for the name of a dish. He'd begun to trust me!

When our eldest son asked for a Dinner Party for his school friends to celebrate his birthday, the dish he wanted was a Rare Hungarian — the red kind, please.

———◆———

There was a time before Elizabeth Bolton cooked, but she finally got to practice when her mother had bursitis in both knees and shoulders. However, there never was a time she didn't tell long, involved stories. "I've never not-written," she says. "As with cooking, practice makes 'practiced' — it's no guarantee of perfection.

The Old Black Cookbook

COOKBOOKS CRAM my kitchen bookcase. The titles change constantly as I replace old volumes with examples that reflect my current culinary interests. But standing tall between newer, more colorful covers is a shabby, spineless, stained, and tattered old volume known in the family as "the old black cookbook." It is the one thing my oldest daughter, Robin, asked for when she got married. It is the one thing I had to deny her, although I later found a copy in an antique store and sent it to her.

It took a while for me to figure out why I couldn't part with it. My mother had given me the cookbook when I got married. Officially titled the *Good Housekeeping Cookbook*, it had taught me most of what I knew about cooking. I could flip it open to any topic without referring to the index. Many of its recipes were old favorites. But my attachment went deeper than that. Family memories, I realized, were stuck to its pages with fruit juice and shortening and sugar, more evocative than any album of photographs. The cookbook was a 25-year chronicle of our lives.

A dozen more years have passed, but the cookbook is still on the shelf. I slip it into my hands, and it falls open to pages that make me smile. Did I ever really need a recipe for pot roast or pork chops? In the earliest days of marriage, of course, we had little money for such luxuries. The festive recipes then included hamburger or chicken or fish, all terribly cheap. Daily fare most often featured rice or macaroni or cheese. A quick flip to the cheese pages, and I am transported to a time before children arrived, to a place far away: to a time and a place where these recipes for Welsh Rabbit and Cheese-Onion Pie were in constant use. And here is the old favorite "payday special" (meaning the day *before* payday) — Baked Cheese Pudding. I see my notations that halve the ingredients to make the recipe suitable for two.

I leap ahead a few pages and a decade of time, and I'm in "eggs" — a section that saw heavy use during the years that my younger daughter, Erin, raised chickens in 40-H. Nearly every recipe on these pages is familiar, from Deviled Eggs to Eggs Divan, from Eggs Foo Yung to omelettes. I flip to the dessert section and find the recipes for eclairs and custards that saved us from total inundation not only by eggs, but by milk. Those were also the years that both girls raised dairy goats.

The kitchen aromas of that period seem to waft from these pages: the sour scent of milk being made into cheese or yogurt; the sweet fruity smells of peaches, blackberries, strawberries, raspberries, or plums, bubbling into jams and jellies; pungent cinnamon and cloves in simmering apple butter; soups and rich stews fragrant with our home-grown tomatoes, corn, peas, snap beans, potatoes, onions, garlic, and herbs; the mouth-watering aroma of baking bread; the savory scent of the spicy ketchup I simmered on the stove all day, half-gone from "sampling" by the time it was done. The old black cookbook was often open on the counter, its pages dusted with flour or spattered with fruit.

The pages of the pie section are among the most soiled and heavily used, a testimonial to holidays with memories encrusted in pumpkin, mince meat and apples. Among the cake recipes I find birthdays, bake sales, grange dinners, potlucks, company meals.

Drop it, and the old black cookbook flops open at the cookie pages. I must have baked these brownies and chocolate chip cookies hundreds of times. My notes run alongside, doubling the ingredients. The page with the huge brown splot was Erin's doing, a spill during her first experiments with baking.

Freezing, canning, carving, converting — I learned them all from this book, and passed what I learned to my daughters. And although I rarely refer to it these days, the old black cookbook has a permanent place on my shelves.

Baked Cheese Pudding

6 BREAD SLICES, CUT INTO 1^1/$_2$" SQUARES
^{1}/$_2$ POUND PROCESS-AMERICAN-CHEESE SLICES
3 EGGS
^{1}/$_2$ TEASPOON SALT
^{1}/$_2$ TEASPOON PAPRIKA
^{1}/$_4$ TEASPOON DRY OR PREPARED MUSTARD
2^1/$_2$ CUPS MILK, OR 1^1/$_4$ CUPS EVAPORATED MILK PLUS 1^1/$_4$ CUPS WATER
FEW SLICES STUFFED OLIVES (OPTIONAL)

Note: substitute cheddar cheese for processed; add chopped onion, bell pepper, dill, or parsley to taste. Heat oven to 325°F.

In greased 1 1/2-quart casserole, arrange alternate layers of bread and cheese, ending with cheese. Beat eggs till frothy; stir in rest of ingredients; pour over cheese. Bake, uncovered, 1 hour. Makes 6 servings. (From *Good Housekeeping Cookbook*: Holt, Rhinehart and Winston, 1955)

Lee C. Kirk, a freelance writer for 25 years, has published hundreds of articles as well as fiction and poetry. A chicken and goat farmer, book store clerk, used book buyer, magazine and newsletter editor, 4-H leader and antique dealer, Lee recently went on-line with her business, The Prints & The Paper, where she sells used and rare books and printed ephemera. http://www.abebooks.com/home/leekirk

Grandpa Always
Got the Burned Cookies

AFTER A WEEK OF RAIN, the tear-drop crystal hanging in my kitchen window finally lured the end of the rainbow into the house. I was teasing a hot cup of water with a tea bag when a narrow shaft of transparent red, yellow and lavender light rested on the old wooden spoon drying in the dish drainer. Four generations had stirred their cookie dough with that spoon, eventually wearing the end flat.

I could still remember the last batch of cookies that Grandma and I had baked together using that spoon. Alzheimer's disease had made it impossible for her to care for herself after Grandpa died. So, she took her most precious belongings and moved into a full-care retirement home.

When I was a little girl, a "special visit" to Grandma's meant "Let's bake cookies!" Now, Grandma needed a special visit to ease her loneliness. I gathered up a few things and drove over the Willamette River and through the woods to Grandmother's apartment.

While I knocked on the door and smiled into the peep hole, I wondered if she would remember me. The door opened slowly. Grandma stood in the doorway wearing a plaid skirt, a pale blue blouse with a tissue tucked in the sleeve, and yellow rubber gloves on both hands. She frowned and I wanted to cry.

"Vicki?" she paused. "Oh! Come in dear!" she said, hugging me without using her hands. "I was cleaning kitty's litter box," her pale cheeks flushed. "I'm so lonely with only Sheeba to talk to."

"Grandma, I'm yours — all day!"

"How delightful! Let me get rid of these gloves." She disappeared into the bathroom.

"Let's bake some cookies, Grandma."

"Oh! I'm so hungry for cookies," she shouted. "But I don't have anything to bake them with anymore," she said as she returned.

"Well, this is your lucky day, Mrs. Davies. I brought everything we need: Grandpa's cookie sheet from WW II Baking School, your mixing bowl, your mother's wooden spoon, AND . . . your famous recipe for Grandma's Drop Cookies. I held up the card like a winning lottery ticket.

A broad smile erased the loneliness on her face. "I was wondering where my things were. You know, I can't find your Grandpa either."

"Look at the time, Grandma," I quickly changed the subject. "We'd better get busy."

Grandma reached into one of the sacks. "Goodness, where did these beautiful walnut meats come from?" she asked.

"The tree in your backyard Grandma," I reminded her gently. "You just forgot."

"I didn't forget!" she snapped. "I just don't remember."

Embarrassed, I asked, "Have you baked anything in your new oven yet?"

"Not even a dot!" she replied curtly.

I tied a red checkered apron around her slender waist and we mixed the ingredients, laughing our way through the mistakes.

"Now, I use one tablespoon of peanut butter with the butter," she instructed and I stirred. But when the cookie dough was thoroughly mixed, she upended the entire bowl onto the cookie sheet.

"Grandma, did you want to make bars?" I asked.

"Ohh — now I remember. Let's make *cookies*!"

From then on, she arranged bit size dough balls on the cookie sheet. Grandma set the timer and we sat down and propped our feet up on her cluttered coffee table. A warm, sweet aroma filled the small room while we looked through a scrapbook bulging with Victorian postcards.

When the timer dinged we peered in "Oh, no!" I gasped. "We burned the cookies!"

Grandma shook her head. "It's all right dear. Your Grandpa Ben always gets the burned cookies anyway. I don't know where he is though."

"He's gone, Grandma." I wrapped my arms around her and wondered if she would remember our afternoon together.

She smiled and began filling the cookie sheet again. "You know dear, lately I start things and can't finish. But today you have given me new life." Grandma slid the second tray into the oven.

While washing our tea cups and cooking utensils, we agreed that those were the best cookies we had ever eaten. Reluctantly, we said our good-byes.

A perfect rainbow arched over the surrounding fir trees when I stepped outside, and for the first time in my life, I knew where the end of the rainbow was.

Grandma's Drop Cookies

2/3 CUP PACKED DARK BROWN SUGAR

1/2 CUP MARGARINE

1/3 CUP PEANUT BUTTER

1 EGG

1 TEASPOON VANILLA

1 TABLESPOON MILK

1 CUP FLOUR

1/2 TEASPOON SODA

1/2 TEASPOON BAKING POWDER

¹/₂ TEASPOON SALT
1 TEASPOON CINNAMON
1 CUP QUICK COOKING OATMEAL
¹/₂ CUP CHOPPED WALNUTS

Heat oven to 350°F. Beat first six ingredients until smooth. Sift dry ingredients. Mix well. Add nuts, mix well. Drop small teaspoons of dough onto lightly oiled baking sheet. Bake 6-7 minutes.

————————

Victoria Tanner is the great granddaughter of founders of the Gresham Outlook, Gresham, Oregon, a graduate in graphic reproduction. She has spent 20 years in litho and flexo printing industries, is a member of the Society of Children's Book Writers and Illustrators, and Oregon Writers Colony. Rocks in My Head *was published in 1976 by Pearl Press.*

A Taste of the 'Real World'

W E KEPT DRIVING and driving, away from our home in Los Angeles and toward the Basque country near Los Banos. No trees, only brown grass and scorching sun. Daddy kept repeating, "Just over the next hill," but the hills rolled on and on. Uncle Steve had invited my parents and me to a picnic so we could visit with him and his new wife, Maria. He said it was time I got a taste of the "real world."

I thought my kindergarten world was just fine, and this didn't look real at all — no stores, no signals, no schools, no houses, nothing but a dirt road. We kept riding along boring brown curves and then almost ran smack into a herd of sheep. I screamed as Daddy jerked off the road, bouncing and fishtailing, sending up clouds of dust. We finally skidded to a stop next to a bunch of junky pickup trucks and colorful blurs of people jumping, laughing and waving like they knew us.

Tents and tables surrounded them, bulging with mountains of food: slabs of roasted meat, thrown onto the table, dripping grease onto the parched dirt; huge wooden bowls of strange looking salads, purples and yellows and greens; whole potatoes, piled high, blackened and smoking; and towering barrels of wine, dripping like the grease. Thick smoke mingled with a band's loud music, bleating sheep, shouting, gun shots and children squealing and chasing each other.

Uncle Steve yanked us from our station wagon and paraded us through his new relatives, making me kiss and hug each one. My face got smashed against scratchy, thick clothes that tickled my nose. Gold necklaces, bracelets and leather belts and holsters bumped against the top of my head. I couldn't really see faces, I just heard strange words and almost choked from the hot bear hugs and thick people smells.

Finally Uncle Steve shouted something to the cooks in Spanish, told me to sit with the other little kids, and shoved my parents off toward the jangling tambourines, guitars and accordions.

A tin dish with chunks of lamb clanged down in front of me, the smell slapping my face and making my eyes and mouth water. I tasted the meat, ignoring the stares and jabberings of the dark children around me. The cooks chattered and grinned down at me. I kept going back for more of the tender lamb, never having tasted anything so good.

"Mas, Senorita?"

"More, please."

Each time I accepted more, the cooks smiled. One of the dirty barefoot boys pointed to my plate and laughed, "Them what hangs between the sheep's legs. It's me job to bite 'em off. Do you still like mas?"

He whispered something to the others who roared with laughter as I jumped up and stumbled backward, face burning. I turned to face a blackened corpse of a lamb turning slowly over the sizzling fire pits, and then another spitted lamb, a glistening brown, and another and another.

I ran toward the deafening band through unfamiliar faces, searching for my parents. Uncle Steve's new relatives were all gyrating, guzzling lunatics. Mommy and Daddy were lost. Two arms grabbed me, flung me in the air and passed me overhead from shoulder to shoulder of the spinning dancers. Grizzly, grimy men pulled at my blond hair, slurring nonsense words. Uncle Steve finally caught me, hugged me and offered me a sheepskin bag of wine.

"Yech, what's it made out of? A stomach?" I puked prairie oysters all over his boots.

A giant lady snatched me and smothered me close to her large sweaty bosom. She murmured things I couldn't understand. I struggled and cried as she lifted me with her strong, garlicy arms and carried me away to sell me. Or hide me forever in her Basque camp. She didn't notice my little fists pounding her. She ignored my screams and finally shoved me through a tent flap where someone else grabbed me before I could get away. I looked up into my Daddy's laughing face and buried myself in his familiar arms.

Prairie Oysters (Hor d'oeuvres)

1 POUND LAMB TESTICLES (8-10 PIECES)
6 CLOVES OF GARLIC, SLICED
1 CUP BUTTER

In a heavy skillet, heat butter on high until brown. Add testicles and garlic. Braise, stirring often, until tender. Serve testicles with toothpicks.

LynneMarie Bain is a freelance writer, counselor and mother. She enjoys books of all types, and anything outdoors.

Thanksgiving 1979

OUR LITTLE FARM provided the bulk of our meat, milk, eggs, garden and orchard produce, but it didn't produce cash, and the sale of eggs, homemade bread and preserves — and the occasional litter of purebred Sheltie puppies — did their part in paying the feed bill. Still there were times when the monthly trip to Prairie Market for flour, sugar and laundry supplies had to be limited to just necessities.

One Thanksgiving I didn't have the spare pennies to buy a little sack of cinnamon "red-hots", my usual seasoning for the baked apples common at this feast. Yet the apples appeared, bright-red, cinnamon-savory and tangy, raisins succulent in their centers.

Eyebrows raised around the table.

"But you said you didn't have any red-hots?"

"I didn't."

Guesses began at how the magic was accomplished. Cinnamon and raisins were easy — they were staples. But what else? What gave it the zest?

"Oh NO!" cried my youngest son.

I grinned, knowing he was right.

It was the thrifty cook's salvation: what else would do the job?

A little zippy juice from a jar of jalepeño peppers, of course.

> . . . *the house steamed with the scent of ham;*
> *There was candied apple, pickled watermelon rind,*
> *Jellies and jams and pumpkin pie and bread:*
> *There would be fourteen at table: all would eat well* . . .

Through the dense packed green of summer,
Weeding the dusty garden with the woods leaning close,
Crowding my view, vine maple shading the orchard,
Water parsed out to the plants, weeds hauled away,

Through the haste of harvest, days growing shorter,
Potatoes dug and dried, heavy squash hauled to the house,
The green tomatoes stored to grow ripe in the dark,
Beans and peas frozen, all the fruits canned,

I waited for this day, a cold morning,
Clouds low and grey over the first snowfall
Mist swirling up through the gap in the frozen pasture
As though sucked here all the way from the sea;

I dressed for the sacrament in warm boots and jacket,
Scarf round my neck and garden fork in hand,
Carrying a basket down through the snow,
Slipping at the garden gate, to the last green rows.

The one enormous carrot weighed two pounds,
Tender and sweet to the core. I pulled one beet.
Two parsnips came where I only intended one;
Chard rising lush in the snow was still summer green.
The snow was stained with the earth from my digging
As I stood and made my prayer in the wintry air:

Such goodness from the soil I labored in!
Such great abundance for my paltry toils!
The feast we eat today was grown right here,
A miracle passed through my simple hands,
Only my time and toil my gift to my family,
All of the rest is the season's gift to me.
This is a holy day. Though trees stand bare:
I can see five mountains through the frosty air.

————————◆————————

*There was a time before Elizabeth Bolton cooked, but she finally got to
practice when her mother had bursitis in both knees and shoulders.
However, there never was a time she didn't tell long, involved stories.
"I've never not-written," she says. "As with cooking, practice makes
'practiced' — it's no guarantee of perfection." This poem appears in the
current edition of the anthology,* In Our Own Voices, *which Elizabeth
edited while serving as president of Oregon Writers Colony.*

Saturday Stress Relief Quiche

THE WASHINGTON COUNTY, Oregon, farms that I visit have names like Persnickety Farm, Smith's Berry Barn, The Spreading Chestnut or Duyck's Peachy Pig Farm. I wait out the long wet winters for them to open in the spring, save up my winter stress and let it flow from me all at once on the first produce run of the year.

I continue my stress relief Saturdays all through the spring, summer, and fall. I drive with the car windows rolled down and the radio off, just me and the peaty smell of rich, black soil; or the mossy fragrance of the meandering muddy river beside the road.

I pull over to the shoulder to let hurried people by, and I pity them their Saturday morning rush, wondering if they even noticed the red-tailed hawk circling lazily above the newly plowed

field, or the pinto colt on wobbly legs, nuzzling its mother for breakfast. I feel blessed to witness such things, and I stop often to watch, or to smell or to listen.

I eavesdrop with my camera, catching a playful, but clumsy newborn alpaca darting between its mother's legs, or the hawk in the top of the roadside tree who allowed me a privileged photo op. I trickle slowly across Jackson Bottom Wetlands, stopping at the roadside viewing area to see which birds are visiting.

In the spring, the pastures of wine-red clover break the endless green of newly sprouted fields, and in the fall the vibrant colors leave me breathless as red and gold flames lick dark-green, forested hillsides.

After a few hours, I go home, with altered attitude and more produce than I can eat. I leave little gifts of food on neighbors' porches, baskets of berries or ears of corn. And I cook, big pots of things that I can warm up during the week, because I hate cooking at the end of a busy workday.

One of my favorite dishes to keep on hand for a quick snack or lunch is a fresh vegetable, crustless, low-fat quiche. Exact amounts and ingredients are not important to this recipe, which is what makes it fun and versatile. Experiment!

Fresh Vegetable, Low-fat Quiche

I use whatever fresh vegetables I have on hand, but my favorite mixture is ZUCCHINI, YELLOW CROOKNECK SQUASH, SWISS CHARD OR SPINACH (about a pound and a half of all vegetables combined). Chop the vegetables and steam them with ¾ OF AN ONION, chopped. Don't overcook. When the vegetables are steamed tender, mash them. Don't puree or put them in a food processor. You want to leave some chunks. I use a potato masher. Let the vegetables cool a while.

Grate 2½-3 CUPS OF CHEESE, SWISS OR CHEDDAR OR A MIXTURE of both. I use low-fat Jarlsberg Swiss (which melts better than most low fat cheeses) when I'm being good, but my favorite is to use a combination of Swiss and sharp cheddar.

Beat 8-12 EGGS (remember amounts are not important, but use more eggs as you add more ingredients) and add them to the cheese. Pour in the veggies and mix it all up.

Put in seasonings to taste. I like GARLIC (you could steam a chopped fresh clove with the vegetables or just use that wonderful already chopped stuff you keep in a jar in the refrigerator), SWEET BASIL, OREGANO AND FRESH GROUND PEPPER. Depending on my mood, I might throw in a ¼ TEASPOON OF LIQUID HOT PEPPER SAUCE (that good clear-your-sinuses kind from Louisiana). Or toss in some CRAB, TUNA, CHICKEN, OR JUST ABOUT ANY KIND OF MEAT (a cup should do fine). I often add a cup of CHOPPED, RAW MUSHROOMS, too. In fact I prefer the mushrooms over the meat any time.

Pour the mixture into a 9x11" baking dish and bake at 325°F until a knife inserted into the center comes out clean, usually ¾ an hour. Can be served warm or cold.

———————

Sue Bronson, a frustrated novelist, is past president of Oregon Writers Colony. Assistant editor for the Home Builders News, Sue writes columns for two monthly newsletters and compiles the "New Releases" column for Writers Northwest newspaper. She'd rather write fiction!

Berries in Suburbia

LEAVING THE FIELD on this cool June morning
the tall quiet lady looked back and said
"I just know heaven will smell like that."
Children with purple smeared lips and scratches
on their sun-burned legs grin as they heft
their small green boxes to the old baby scale.

Neighbors from the *cul de sac* between here
and the brand new school roll their eyes
when Stevie tells them to look for the deer tracks
in front of row fifteen, but we watch them stooping,
motioning Come! to the ladies on row nine.
Mr. Swanson, who picks for jam
for his doctor daughters told us he saw two
quail as he walked across the field, told us
when he was a boy he'd hunt quail with his dad,
told us he'd be back.

Its really time to close the field, let the berries
ripen, but the last car in brought a basket fitted
with plastic jars. The lady was going to fill them,
carry the basket on her lap to her son in Arizona.
And a woman stops on her way home from work,
says she moved here because of her friend's berry cobbler,
picks a big bowl so she can make her own.

I hesitate. Long days in February rain culminate
in this short season, this small patch. I'll let them pick.
This van is from Texas, the man, with an Intel name tag,
says he'll be back, bring his children, he wants them
to "experience what they left home for." And this lady,
her mother next to her with a fresh-patched eye, I let
park in the shade. She only wants enough for a pie.

Boysenberry Cobbler

Major hint — if making in a round cake or casserole NEVER
cover the center! Everything else will burn before the center gets
done. My favorite cobbler is made with a commercial baking mix

from a box. Its very quick, very easy and always very good. These are for 8 or 9" round pans; for 9x13" pan, double everything.

FRESH
4 CUPS BERRIES
4 TABLESPOONS BAKING MIX
3/4 CUPS SUGAR
1/2 TEASPOON CINNAMON

Mix and pour into buttered pan, dot with butter.

FROZEN
2 1/2-3 CUPS BERRIES AND JUICE
4 TABLESPOONS BAKING MIX
3/4 CUPS SUGAR
1/2 TEASPOON CINNAMON

Mix in saucepan, stir until it boils and thickens. Pour into buttered pan, dot with butter.

Mix 1 cup baking mix, 1/3 cup milk, 1 tablespoon sugar and 1/4 teaspoon cinnamon to a soft dough. Drop by forkfuls around pan (probably 6 or 7 biscuits . . . none in center). Bake at 425°F until its center bubbles; 10-12 minutes. Perfect for Sunday brunch with milk or cream; great dessert with ice cream.

Berry Haiku and Recipe

Jello, hot water,
fresh frozen berries:
July in January

1 LARGE BOX BERRY FLAVORED GELATIN
2 CUPS BOILING WATER

Stir to dissolve.

ADD 1 QUART FRESH-FROZEN BERRIES
(RASPBERRY, BOYSENBERRY, BLACK OR BLUE)

Stir just til it begins to jell. Refrigerate an hour or more. Enjoy!

———◆———

Sharon Roso married into Boysenberries in 1961. She has been involved with poetry not nearly so long, studying with Oregon Writers Colony workshops, at Haystack and the Yachats Literary Festival, all in Oregon. She is a grandmother and a happy new student at Marylhurst College in Portland, Oregon.

Emma's Penny

HER APRON STRINGS TIE GENERATIONS TOGETHER, threading our common ground, mothers, daughters, grand-daughters, from wood stoves to microwaves. She calls her apron a "penny," a term her mother used as a pioneer's child at the foot of the Canadian Rockies. No doubt once it was "pinnie," derived from "pinafore," with a regional accent. I can't see an apron anymore without remembering her deft fingers tying that bow with swift and efficient strokes as she begins sacred preparation of food that nourished my childhood soul.

And now, as she rests fitfully in the nursing home, curled up like a little girl, her smooth silver hair is a gossamer nest of memory for me. After 90 years, her face is still nearly wrinkle free and her sapphire eyes, when they look into mine, light a path back to my roots of comfort in the kitchen. It's where I remember her best, stirring porridge on the wood stove, kneading bread on the plank table, peeling garnet apples from the backyard tree.

My grandmother looks up from her pillow and, knowing she should recognize me but not sure if I'm her sister or her mother, asks, "Have you finished picking the cherries yet?"

Her voice carries centuries of knowing. I nod, "Yes, Grama, they're ripe and juicy and ready for pie."

She looks at me with more than a little consternation. "Well, little girl, you'd better get busy before Harry gets home. And don't forget to put your penny on." I nod, tears welling at the injustice I feel, for old age has robbed me now.

We go on to talk about how hard my grampa Harry works, how many potatoes should we cook, and is that scrawny chicken going to be enough to feed the crew.

We are interrupted by the present. The nurse whose large shadow looms over my grandmother's tiny body, waits for us to finish and says, "Emma? It's time for your bath." My grandmother tells her in no uncertain terms that she's doing just fine the way she is and with a shake of her crooked finger, announces that she's going home. "Just as soon as this leg is better, I'll be able to go home again and I'll take a bath in my own tub." She looks at me for confirmation.

The stroke has paralyzed her left side now and there's no hope of her going home. "Yes, Grama," I say, "soon you'll be going home."

She drifts off, sleeping an infant's innocent drowse. I watch her face for signs of dreams and memories; I try to pull her back to me. As I stroke her thin hand, translucent as the skin of a spring onion, I remember the heart of her kitchen, her "penny" tied with a bow, and the verdant aromas of simple food bubbling on the stove. Now the disinfectant smells of the hospital room betray this memory. And, here there is no glow from the fire to warm her .

She wakes up again and greets me anew. "Well, I didn't know you were here. How was the ride? Did you put the horses out?" I tell her yes, and that the ride was fine. I ask her if there's anything she needs. Her eyes pierce mine. She knows something's amiss but she can't quite figure it out.

"Oh I had the most awful piece of pie for lunch. They don't know how to make mincemeat here so they gave me a bite of an apple pie they must have found in the road." The connection of food to the soul of our family is still very much alive in her mind. Especially when it comes to pie. I remember her mincemeat jars, filled to the brim, and spilling their contents into buttery crusted pies. Pies, round as ripe fruit on the tree, dusted with love, and heaping with autumn's harvest.

"The boys have gone hunting again," she tells me. "Maybe they'll bring back a deer and we can grind some neck meat for pie." I can't answer her now because the love I feel for her has silenced my voice. "You keep an eye out for them," she admonishes me.

Grama gestures out the window to the mountain road only she sees, "They'll be home before sundown and our dinner should be ready by then." Sleep comes again slowly, as it does every few minutes now, and she's gone to her other world.

I pull out the letter from my purse, and reading it, I'm amazed that we're talking about this. It's a letter she wrote to my mother many years ago. Its contents tell a story about what she cooked that day, and what the sky looked like, about the bend of a tree in the wind, and how she hoped the winter didn't settle in too soon. She writes her tale in rounded letters and says she's enclosed "that recipe you wanted."

Words swim across the page, merging together with my own salty memories. My tear seasons this page and my grandmother awakens again. "Oh Linda," she says with a grin, "there's nothing left to cry about." She remembers me again and I know that as long as I live in that tiny space in her mind, for now anyway, the world feels safe and secure.

"Grama," I say, "I have to go now. It's time to make that pie." I bend to kiss her soft and tender cheek, the one with roses in it. She pats my hand, her mouth curling in a wry smile and whispers in my ear, "Don't forget to put your penny on."

Emma's Mincemeat

Now this mincemeat is a hodge podge. You can use hamburger if you boil it in a chunk and grind it again because if you put vinegar and etc. on it raw, it stays crumbly and won't blend.

Now . . . .

Grind a pile of meat. I make a pile in my big preserving pot, rounded up under my hands. Then RAISINS AND CURRENTS, same size pile. Then CHOPPED APPLES, a little more than both. Sometimes, I put PEEL in it, maybe some RED CHERRIES, but not very often. Pour on about a QUART OF VINEGAR, maybe more. Add some WATER, about half and half. BROWN SUGAR to taste. Also, CINNAMON, CLOVES, AND NUTMEG. Add some SALT.

Cook and stir and taste and add until it tastes OK. It will be on the tart side while hot but not too much. I seal hot in sterile jars. Hope you can figure this out but it's the way mama made hers. If the kids get any game, the neck makes the nicest mincemeat.

———◆———

Linda Marie Nygaard is a Portland writer and cook. Her work has been published nationally and internationally in magazines and newspapers; she wrote the guidebook CitySmart: Portland *(John Muir Publications, 1996). Linda's passion for food and home cooking has led to publication in The Oregonian's FoodDay and Walking magazine. Born and raised on a ranch in Montana, Linda's work has taken her to Australia, Guatemala, Belize, Mexico, France and Switzerland. But one of her favorite destinations continues to be Colonyhouse at Rockaway Beach, Oregon, where salt seasons the air and Mother Sea sharpens her skills.*

Amish Country, Rivel Soup
and a Good-bye Kiss

WHEN I WAS FOURTEEN, everyone knew within two days that I was the new student who came to school in a private, 30-seat Army bus. My father had just returned to the military and was executive officer of the weapons storage facility at Letterkenny Ordinance Depot. I was the only teenager on base and commuted to a public high school in Chambersburg, Pennsylvania.

But in the heart of the Amish country, my drab-colored, military conveyance couldn't match those wonderful horse-drawn buggies gliding down the roadways past barns painted with hex signs. Or the Saturday markets filled with mouthwatering aromas of Amish shoo-fly pie and stacks of yummy pastries, all miraculously cooked without electricity. Or the most gorgeous classmate I'd ever seen: a blond Grace Kelly in black Amish dress and pin-tucked organdy cap.

The school also came equipped with my first boyfriend, Duane Gooch, whose mother made rivel soup. As I recall, our fathers worked together. Mr. Gooch, a civilian employee, invited my parents and me for a regional-style dinner. I don't recall much of that evening, only their son and the first course, rivel soup.

Raised on my mother's Italian food and my father's Tennessee preferences, my pallet was more used to a full-bodied spaghetti or cornbread and fried okra, though I never could down a serving of the cold pickled pigs feet Daddy relished. But Italian or Southern, we were instantly hooked on this Amish specialty.

Mrs. Gooch told us how to make the soup, but for some reason Mother never wrote the recipe down, nor could she duplicate it. I had better luck with Duane.

We dated in my own fourteen-year-old version: Sundays at the Officer's Club swimming pool, phone calls, football games and shy smiles accompanied with quick conversations in the high school hallways.

But our dating was brief. Four months later, my father was transferred to the Presidio in San Francisco, California, and we were off once more. Duane and his parents came to say good-bye. While our folks visited in the living room, we sat on the floor in the sunroom as I packed the family books, including *Lady Chatterley's Lover,* one I'd had strict orders not to read. Duane's awkward

groping, off-target kisses and prickly upper lip bore small resemblance to Lady Chatterley's experiences.

The years passed. My memory of the soup fared better than Duane's kisses, so I continuously searched for the elusive rivel. And one day in a cookbook I saw it: rivel soup.

I faithfully followed the recipe and served the soup to my family along with its history — Duane carefully excised because of five pairs of tender ears. But, no! It couldn't be rivel soup — it tasted dishwater-bland as Duane's kisses! My family endured three or four experiments as I struggled to recreate my gastronomic memory — no easy task with four sons who masqueraded as eating machines. Until success.

A rivel soup more tantalizing and tasty than a good-bye kiss.

Rivel Soup

CHICKEN BROTH

2 QUARTS (OR MORE) OF WATER SEASONED WITH:
1 BAY LEAF
1 CHOPPED ONION
SALT AND PEPPER TO TASTE
1 CHICKEN, CUT-UP OR PARTS OF YOUR CHOICE (COOKED IN THE WATER)
1 CAN OF WHOLE KERNEL CORN, DRAINED

RIVELS

1 CUP FLOUR
1 TEASPOON SALT
1 EGG

Wash and cut up chicken, put in water and bring to a boil. Skim the foam from the water as it returns to a boil. Add seasonings and cook until tender. Bone chicken, dice or shred and return to the broth. Add corn.

Just before serving, make the rivels. Mix flour and salt together in a small bowl. Make a well in the center of the flour and drop in the egg. Mix the egg into the flour with a fork until pea-sized nuggets form. These are the rivels. Bring soup broth to a boil and scatter the rivels through your fingers into the boiling liquid while stirring to prevent clumping. Cook 10 minutes. Serves 6.

**This soup does not keep for reheating as the rivels congeal when cold.

———————

Sandra Millett, author, lecturer and fiber artist, is an enthusiastic spokesperson for Romance Writers of America(RWA) and has been a working member of six RWA chapters. She has had two editions of Quilt-As-You-Go *published. She was secretary for the Beaverton City Library site committee and appointed to Beaverton's library advisory board. Married for 38 years, Sandra manages her husband's law office, is the mother of five sometimes-adult children and a retired registered nurse.*

Journal Entry: 16 May 1992

Full Moon of Vesak, Buddhist Celebration of Enlightenment. Borobudur Temple, Central Java, Indonesia — An amber sun, batiks of gold and brown, faces of sienna. Beneath a canopy of cane and palms young mothers held babies to breast, pensive old men sipped hot tea from glasses, and laughing youths bartered clove cheroots.

JOHN HELD MY HAND while we sat at a table and watched a woman stir a wok of gado gado, a peanut sauce, and vegetables, over a makeshift gas bottle stove. A passing tourist offered to take our picture and I gave her my camera. Flash. Snap. The moment immortalized.

We were alone in the crowd. In his eyes I could believe he was the only man in the world and I was the only woman. Only man, only woman, the written words look tired, bankrupt, but how else to describe the feeling of being magic? Dinner arrived and we ate slowly, smiled, giggled, spoke in sentences finished by shared thoughts, a feast enchanted by heaven.

At sunset we joined 10,000 others in the processional walk to the temple gates. The sunset became shadows, the air was rich with devotion and night jasmine. Guarding the southern sky were the Menorah Mountains, north was Mount Merapo, northeast was Mount Merbabu, and in the center of the plateau lay the temple of Borobudur.

"If we become separated," he said, "Trust that I will find you. Always. Trust yourself. Trust me." His lips touched mine, the gossamer of a dragonfly, two breaths, one spirit.

We entered as the electric lights were switched on, momentarily flooding the temple grounds in blinding white. On the south lawn we found a place and sat as the lights dimmed.

The old monk began the story of the Buddha Shakyamuni's enlightenment beneath the Bodhi tree. The narrative was in Bahasa, the language of Indonesia. John whispered the first sentences in English, then said almost sternly, "Now, stop trying to translate, feel the words and you will understand." And I did.

The moon climbed the sky. The monk called for silence and the contemplation of motivation. Why was I here? For the enlightenment of all sentient beings. What did I hope to gain for myself? Nothing, there was nothing more to wish for.

With 10,000 people I closed my eyes and prayed for peace, all souls, all worlds, one consciousness. In a vision the Buddha appeared above my head and before me, behind him sacred Mount Meru. The face of Buddha, the face of man. The electric lights were turned off and the vision of Buddha became a rain of lotus blossoms blessing all existence. The moon reached over the dome spire of the closed main stupa and moonlight burned through the diamond shaped windows of surrounding domes; in one voice we offered all that has been given, that all may return to perfection.

Near midnight it was time to go, four hours had passed since the ceremony began . . . . At the hotel John stood behind me on the balcony and we watched the moon until it became the sun. The smell of him freshly bathed, the feeling of being so close without touching; he wore the sarong I'd bought him in Soho and the ring of spiraled silver I'd made years before with a prayer that I'd see him again.

We lay on the bed to sleep, he with his arm under my neck and his hand at the small of his back, I with the weight of the white linen dress I still wore, wanting to take it off, but not daring to move. "I had a vision of a mountain," he said, his voice hushed in a gentle New Zealand accent, "every step is the path." I raised to see him, to say that I too had seen the mountain. "Shh," he said, eyes closed. "I know," he smiled, "Lie back down, listen to my heart, let it take you into sleep, into dreams."

— *from a work in progress,* The Spiral Path

Gado Gado (Peanut Sauce)

Can be served warm or cold as a party dip with vegetables, a salad dressing, or stir fry. Goes well with a glass of port, an old photograph, a bouquet of jasmine, and a prayer for enlightenment.

1/2 CUP PEANUT BUTTER (CHUNKY OR CREAMY)
1/2 CUP HONEY
1/2 TEASPOON CHINESE FIVE SPICE
2 TABLESPOONS SWEET CHILI-GARLIC SAUCE
2 TEASPOON SESAME SEEDS AND 1 TEASPOON OF SESAME OIL

Stir ingredients together, microwave for one minute, and serve.

———————◆———————

Morgan Escalante is a retired broadcast journalist with 10 years of experience working in the Middle East and Southeast Asia. She now lives in Oregon with her husband and teenage children, Steinbeck the parrot, Maya the cat, and three goldfish — F. Scott, Zelda, and Gertrude. Between raising and writing, she practices Buddhism, teaches meditation, and assists others through past-life regression hypnosis. She's 39 years old.

Piccalilli

NOT THE SPRING BUT THE AUTUMN is the real time of beginnings, at least it is in our culture based on the academic year. The year always began for me when school started. It still does. It's the time of evocative smells: pencil wood and new books, wet leaves on the wet earth, the smoke of the new fire in the grate, foods cooking for hours. It's a time of rich, new color: the salmons and yellows replacing the graying greens of the summer, the rapid flushing of the monotonous blue sky with the dramatic, battle gray of the storm clouds. Everything is being shaken to its core; shaken out of its hot sun lethargy. It's time to pick and store and dig again. That's probably the reason why I grasp the season with vigor. New ideas crop up. New energies emerge. New hope explodes. And old memories slide up into my consciousness like the smell from the pot of green tomatoes simmering in vinegar sliding up my nose, the piccalilli.

The term "comfort food" is one that everyone knows and interprets in the remembrance of childhood. For many people comfort food is something warm and salt and savory with a texture of swallowing porridge. For me it is different. It is the edge of piquancy, the bite of vinegar followed by the healing kiss of sugar and the crunch of unripened tomatoes — piccalilli. The word has no distinct origins, and the recipe has no holy ingredients. It is a word and food of personal taste and comfort.

After years of staring out at the back yard and imagining potatoes, tomatoes, melons, lettuce and green beans, this year I finally planted Roma tomatoes. It's now the end of the brilliant red crop and there are dozens of greens hanging too late for the sun to ripen them. I bring in about eight quarts, and they sit there on the kitchen counter for the days it takes me to gather up the all the vinegar, sugar, salt, celery and mustard seed that I need. Then of course there's the equipment, the jars, the lids, the huge pots.

This was a food of our childhood, always popping into conversations at family reunions when we'd remember the good times with our parents, Charley and Eileen. We were always oddballs, our family, calling our parents by their first names.

"Remember the piccalilli they used to make?"

"Yeah, that was great stuff."

"How come nobody makes it anymore?"

It went with all the other, more traditional comfort foods, the Thanksgiving and Christmas turkeys, the home baked beans, the hot dogs and hamburgers. It was the bitter and the sweet that every meal needs, and every family. It was, and is, a reminder of my mother and father bent together over a project like Thanksgiving dinner. The connection between them, so often scratched and bleeding from their arguments over money or kids, was warm and close at those times, and that was comfort for me as well as for

them. The same comfort I would feel listening to them from my bed early in the morning before my father went off to work. They would laugh at the morning radio, and talk about the news, and be quiet every few minutes for what I knew was their affection. They didn't show it much when we were around, but I saw the traces of it sometimes. Like the times when my mother would look up from the kitchen sink and sigh "Oh, Charley" with a piccalilli mixture of love and pain.

And that was comfort indeed, the comfort of knowing that at its core life was safe, and there was love and protection in those two people chopping tomatoes and onions and peppers and boiling glass jars together.

So here I am trying to reinvent comfort by making the food. I have one full day to do it, no more. It's all here in front of me. Two large white enamel pots holding a mix of *8 QUARTS OF CHOPPED GREEN TOMATOES, 6 LARGE ONIONS CUT INTO THIN HALF SLICES, 6 GREEN PEPPERS* and *1 RED ONE* cut into short strips. The mix has sat overnight covered in a *10 PERCENT SALT BRINE*. Waiting in another large pot is a ½ *GALLON OF CIDER VINEGAR* with *8 CUPS OF SUGAR* dissolved in it. Beside this is a bowl with *4 TABLESPOONS EACH* of *WHOLE BLACK PEPPERCORNS, WHOLE MUSTARD AND CELERY SEED, 4 CINNAMON STICKS* and *1 TABLESPOON OF WHOLE CLOVES*.

The hard work part is the sterilizing. Boiling each jar and lid for ten minutes then draining them. I remember the occasional snap from my father, "Don't touch the rim of the jar with your fingers!"

Now is the time, the ritual, the conjuring of the memory, the cooking. The mixture, drained of brine then rinsed three times, is covered in the sweetened vinegar. The spices, divided into two piles and tied in muslin bags, are buried in the middle of the two eight quart enamel pots. The gas is turned on low and the smells slowly gather and fill the house, as the mixture comes slowly to the boil and simmers for a quarter of an hour. But the evocation will last much longer than this. It will coat the walls with the warmth of decades ago in that chaotic and loving house in Cambridge, Massachusetts. The jars, full of green and red, coolness and warmth, acid and honey, spice and sugar, screaming and love, will sit on my kitchen shelf for a couple of weeks, till their contents have grown in wisdom, age and grace. Then they'll go out to the family to be a reminder of the place, the origin of comfort.

Joe Cronin, a Portland poet, writer, and actor was born in Boston and lived in a variety of countries and careers before settling in Oregon 17 years ago. He has lived in Chicago; Yorkshire, England; and the highlands of Scotland. He has been a research chemist, a gardener, the host of a radio poetry program, an actor with the Oregon Shakespeare Festival, and a member of the Portland Slam Poetry Team. His work has appeared in the Rain City Review and he is author of the book The Next Time I See This Place, I'll Have a Better Seat. *Joe is currently at work on two new books of poetry due out in early 1999.*

Leave Me, Leave My Cheesecake

———

ITS THE LITTLE THINGS you miss in a divorce . . . like cheese-cake. Never mind the kids, the house, the romance, the sex, my ex missed my cheesecake. And when he discovered that the new girlfriend was ignorant of culinary arts and he had to learn to cook if they were going to eat, he begged me for the recipe.

"Sorry bub! Leave me, leave my cheesecake."

"Please! We're having a party."

"Try Jello."

It's not that I'm vindictive, or mean-spirited. My cheesecake is special. It's something that I do well. Why should I share it with the likes of him?

And so it went for several years. He tried end runs around me to friends he thought had the recipe (not many did). Those few who did knew better than to share it, especially with him.

He even rifled my recipe files once when he came to pick up the kids and I wasn't home. The dog-eared, vanilla-splattered card wasn't in the fat, red three-ring binder where I kept recipes in plastic sleeves. Gee, you'd think a guy I'd been married to for 17 years would remember that I never put things where they belong.

He didn't win until a few years later at the office Christmas party we had for our employees at my home (I'd remained in business with him for three years after our divorce, but that's another story). The girlfriend still didn't know the difference between boiling and baking, but he'd become a decent cook by trial and error (like finding out from his ex-wife that one clove of garlic meant one of the little buds, not the whole cluster. This after the spaghetti had already been served to his guests.)

So, in he came with the hot spiced wine; I swear to God, the best I'd ever tasted — and that determination was made before I'd had way more than my share.

"Where'd you get the recipe?" I asked.

"None of your business."

"Come on!"

"Trade you." The grin was absolutely malevolent.

"No! Not my cheesecake!"

"Sorry," he said with a shrug.

"Oh, okay."

So, here they are, the hot spiced wine and infamous cheesecake.

Hot Spiced Wine

1/2 GALLON OF BURGUNDY
1/2 GALLON OF APPLE CIDER
1/2 CUP OF LEMON JUICE
1 CUP OF SUGAR (OR TO TASTE)
6 3"-STICKS OF CINNAMON
1 TABLESPOON WHOLE CLOVES
1 TABLESPOON ALLSPICE BERRIES
LEMON SLICES (OPTIONAL)

Heat all ingredients except lemon slices in microwave or on top of the stove, stirring occasionally until sugar is dissolved and mixture is hot, not boiling. Transfer to a crock pot to keep at serving temperature. Add optional lemon slices. Mixture can be started in a crockpot, but it will take much longer.

Sue's Cheesecake (or pie)

I bake this in a large glass pie pan rather than a spring form pan because I like a thick, crisp buttery graham cracker crust.

CRUST

15 GRAHAM CRACKERS, CRUSHED FINE
1/3 CUP BUTTER (USE THE REAL STUFF, IT'S WORTH IT)
1/4 CUP SUGAR
(OR CHEAT, AND USE PACKAGED GRAHAM CRACKER CRUMBS AND FOLLOW THE RECIPE ON THE BOX)

Mix well and press the mixture into a deep 10" glass pie pan. The crust should be a little less than 1/4" thick. Don't use more than you need. Leftover crumb mixture can be refrigerated and used for something else.

FILLING

16 OUNCES OF CREAM CHEESE, SOFTENED TO ROOM TEMPERATURE (DO NOT USE WHIPPED, PRESOFTENED OR LOW FAT CREAM CHEESE.)
3 EGGS, BEATEN
1 CUP OF SUGAR
2 TEASPOONS VANILLA
1 TEASPOON LEMON JUICE

Beat all of the above until light and frothy. Pour into prepared crust and bake at 350°F for about 25 minutes. Ovens vary, so watch closely. If the center seems to still be jiggly, bake a little longer. Remove from the oven and cool for 7 or 8 minutes. Prepare topping.

TOPPING

1¹/₄ CUPS SOUR CREAM
5 TEASPOONS SUGAR
1¹/₄ TEASPOONS VANILLA

Very gently spread the topping over the top of the cheesecake evenly to the edges. Be careful not to break the top, which should have formed a slight crust while cooling. Return to the oven and bake for 10 more minutes. Cool an hour or so to room temperature then chill in the refrigerator for 6 hours before serving.

Note: I'm a cheesecake purist, so I don't top my cheesecakes with fruity toppings or syrups. On a rare occasion I've decorated the top with thin slices of kiwi, which make an attractive display. I also prefer basic vanilla flavored cheesecake with just a little lemon, but by all means, try other flavorings to suit your tastes.

———————◆———————

Sue Bronson, a frustrated novelist, is past president of Oregon Writers Colony. She's the assistant editor for the Home Builders News, writes columns for two monthly newsletters and compiles the "New Releases" column for Writers Northwest newspaper. She'd rather write fiction!

The Goldwater Frijoles

W HEN OUR CHILDREN WERE YOUNG, we lived on a rocky hillside in Paradise Valley. Cresting that hill was the glass and rock house of Arizona's favorite son, Barry Goldwater.

Rusty, our youngest at six, greatly admired Barry Goldwater, mainly because of his efforts to keep housing developments off our nearby and beloved landmark Camelback Mountain.

On warm spring day just before lunch, Rusty announced he'd climb the hill and visit "Barry." I argued that Senator Goldwater probably wasn't home, and if he were, the chances of getting through the gate and onto his property were slim. I couldn't bear to think of Rusty's eagerness turning to disappointment over making the long, hot climb and finding the big gate closed and locked to visitors. Kids can't walk right up to the front door of the most famous man in Arizona and expect to barge in, I told myself. One look, however, at Rusty's beaming face and dripping red hair still showing ridges from his comb, made me shut up. Let him learn the realities of life in his own way. "Mind your manners," was all I said.

After Rusty raced out the door I stewed, thinking of rattlesnakes hiding from the sun under rocks. I worried about the steep climb. The heat. An hour later, Rusty reappeared, all sweaty and humming a tune. He shot past me and went upstairs. I followed, hoping he'd volunteer a report. He made a side trip to the bathroom and when he came out I could stand it no longer.

"Well?" I said.

"What?"

"What happened?"

"Oh," he said, as though not noticing I followed him around like the family dog. "It was hard climbing the hill. All those rocks. And it was hot."

"And — ?" I prompted.

"There was this old white-haired guy working on the gate up there at Goldwater's. I decided to talk to him first and find out if they were home. He was pretty busy but nice. Said they were home. I asked him if they ever had company. He said they had lots of company. I sat on a rock and we talked for a while. I told him I liked how Barry kept houses off Camelback Mountain. I was chicken to ask if I could go to the house, so I asked him if he worked for Barry

Goldwater. He said he *was* Barry Goldwater. He took me to his radio shack and we talked to France on the ham radio. He took me into the house and gave me some chili stuff. It was pretty neat."

And then Rusty went to his room and fed his goldfish. So much for the realities of life.

———

According to the Phoenix Junior League cookbook, the following recipe is Peggy Goldwater's Arizona Frijoles. I have always wondered if maybe this is the "chili stuff" they fed Rusty that day some 30 years ago.

Goldwater's Arizona Frijoles

2 POUNDS PINTO BEANS
2 TEASPOONS SALT
2 LARGE ONIONS, CHOPPED
3 CLOVES GARLIC, MASHED
1 4-OUNCE CAN CHOPPED GREEN CHILIES
1 CAN TACO SAUCE
1 28-OUNCE CAN TOMATOES
1/2 TEASPOON CUMIN SEED
1/2 TEASPOON BLACK PEPPER

Soak pinto beans in cold water overnight. Drain, wash and cover with about 2" water. Add salt and boil over moderate heat for about an hour, adding water if needed. Add onion, garlic, chilies, taco sauce, tomatoes, cumin seed and pepper. Cook over reduced flame for 1-2 hours until beans are tender. These frijoles may be converted into a delicious chili con carne by the addition of chopped beef (2 pounds) sauteed until brown with a chopped onion, and added to the beans after the first hour of cooking. Serves 10.

———

Martha Miller, former executive director of The American Institute of Architects in Arizona, moved to the green hills of Portland three years ago. She spends her time writing short stories, endlessly revising a novel, and leading the Oregon Writers Colony board as president.

Baking Day in Canada

SATURDAY MORNING — baking day. By the time we got to the kitchen, the big black range was blazing. The room was toasty warm, with the smell of good things in the works.

In the 1930s few women worked outside the home. Like most homemakers of that era, women in our village slavishly followed a rigid schedule.

Monday — washday. Neighbors competed to see who could get the wash on the line earliest in the morning. I can see my mother looking across the field, remarking, "There's Mrs. Guy — first again!"

Tuesday — ironing. Everything needed ironing; wash-and-wear fabrics and no-iron sheets had yet to be developed. Early electric

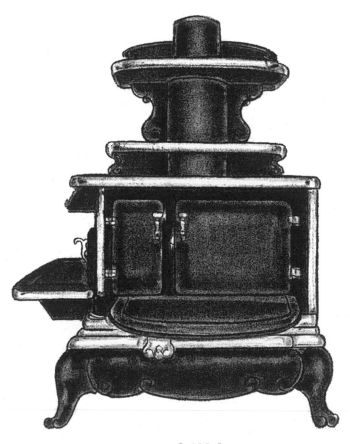

irons had no thermostats, so it took skill and a great deal of practice to avoid scorching clothes by unplugging the iron at the right time, then replugging it as the iron cooled. (My English mother called it "ion" — and so did I, until I was teased. Then I put a strong "r" in it, until it sounded like "I run," and I was teased again, so I changed to "I earn." I'm not sure I've got it right yet. I prefer to avoid the word as well as the task.)

Wednesday — mending or knitting for the Red Cross.

Thursday — ladies' meeting at the church. They wore dresses, hats and gloves in all weather — dark in winter; white in summer.

Friday — cleaning. We would arrive home for lunch to shouts of "Take off those shoes," and step onto a freshly washed kitchen floor covered in newspapers. This was also grocery delivery day: shopping orders were picked up on Wednesday, and the groceries delivered on Friday, at no extra charge.

On Saturday, we made our own breakfasts while Mum baked and made dessert for Sunday — that was the only day we had that treat. Mother seldom baked cakes: she found it difficult to keep a steady temperature on the old wood-burning stove, so her cakes often fell flat — in spite of her admonishments to us: "Don't slam the door;" and "Don't stomp on the floor." Some of our favorites were pig-in-a-blanket (sausage rolled in pastry), lemon meringue pie, or butter tarts (she called them buttah tahts).

My sister and I loved to get the bits of leftover pastry. We rolled it out and sprinkled it with raisins to make "fly cemeteries."

Sometimes, instead of pastries, Mum made cornstarch puddings, blanc mange, or jelly. Sheriff's jelly packets came with a "flavor bud" that looked and tasted like candy. My brother and I once were spanked for eating the flavor buds from four jelly packets while Mum was hanging out the wash.

No one worked or played on Sunday. Stores were closed. Mum cooked only one meal that day. We got our own breakfasts, lifting the lid of the wood stove to toast bread on a fork over the flames. Mum served dinner at 1:30; usually roast beef, mashed potatoes, peas, and Yorkshire pudding with gravy. Then, with bellies fed, we went to Sunday School to feed our souls.

I close my eyes. I am back in the big toasty kitchen, sitting at the old farmhouse table. Its much-mended tablecloth is set with dishes that don't match: dinner plates, bread-and-butter plates, cups and saucers. We must eat the English way; lifting fork to mouth with the left hand, knife at the ready in the right, and must never reach, but ask politely — and "No laughing at the table!"

I struggle through the main course, for I won't get dessert unless I eat it. Then comes the treat — butter tarts!

My teeth assault the crisp pastry, allowing the syrupy center to glide sweetly over my tongue, caressing each plump raisin as I roll the ambrosial mixture around my mouth, savoring the taste, anticipating the next bite . . . a-a-a-h. Heaven!

Canadian Butter Tarts

Make pastry sufficient for 16 medium-size tart shells.

FILLING
1 CUP RAISINS
1 TEASPOON VANILLA
1 CUP BROWN SUGAR
LUMP OF BUTTER (ABOUT 1 TABLESPOON)
1 EGG, WELL BEATEN
2 TABLESPOONS DARK CORN SYRUP
PINCH OF SALT
(IF DESIRED, 1/2 CUP CHOPPED WALNUTS MAY BE ADDED, ALTHOUGH THIS IS NOT TRADITIONAL)

Method: The secret of this recipe is to be sure that the raisins are well soaked in hot water. Pour boiling water on raisins and let stand for about 15 minutes. Drain well. To the warm raisins, add butter, brown sugar, beaten egg, salt, and vanilla. Add chopped walnuts if desired.

Fill tart shells a little more than half full. Bake at 450°F on bottom rack for 5 minutes. Reduce heat to 400°F and bake an additional 10-15 minutes. Filling should be slightly runny, although some people prefer it cooked a little firmer.

Jean Bradley, an Oregon Writers Colony board member, is a retired journalist and public relations executive whose short stories have been published in the U.S.A. and Canada. She has received writing awards from Willamette Writers, Oregon Press Women and the Public Relations Society of America. Her book-length memoir, A Home Across the Water, *won awards from Oregon Press Women and the National Federation of Press Women.*

From a Polish Kitchen

BOTH OF MY PARENTS left Poland during the great immigration of 1912 and settled in a Polish neighborhood in Cleveland, Ohio. Papa woke up every morning at 4:30 to catch a street car for his job as a laborer in a cement factory. Mama also would get up to fix him a hearty breakfast of salt pork and fried eggs. While he was stowing this away, she prepared two or three thick meat sandwiches and a pint whiskey bottle of coffee for his lunch.

My earliest memories are of Mama cooking wonderful soups and thick stews using the fresh cabbage and beets from her backyard garden. I am including a recipe for bigos which I feature in my Polish dinners for friends and family. A Polish housewife would use whatever game her husband brought home from a day of hunting in the forests. I have also used elk meat or venison when available instead of beef.

Easy Hunter's Stew (Bigos)

1 TEASPOON PAPRIKA
1 TEASPOON SALT
1/2 TEASPOON PEPPER
1/4 CUP FLOUR
1/4 POUND OF CHOPPED BACON OR SALT PORK
1 POUND OF CUBED BEEF
1 POUND OF CUBED PORK
12 OUNCE KIELBASA OR SMOKED SAUSAGE CUT IN 1" SLICES
1/2 POUND OF FRESH MUSHROOMS
1 CUP CHOPPED ONION
1 CUP CHOPPED APPLE
1 CUP OF DRY RED OR WHITE WINE (I USE DRY VERMOUTH)
22-OUNCE JAR OF SAUERKRAUT

Fry bacon or salt pork over medium heat until crisp in heavy Dutch oven or stew pot. Remove with slotted spoon, chop and reserve. Dredge pork and beef in flour and seasoning mixture and brown in bacon drippings, stirring frequently. Add 1 cup of chopped onion and wine. Simmer until meat is tender. Add sauerkraut, chopped mushrooms, apple and kielbasa. Cook 30 minutes longer. Serve with rye bread and potatoes. I usually present this in a Polish casserole and ladle out individual servings into large soup bowls at the table. I garnish each bowl with reserved bacon and a dollop of sour cream.

Dorothy Prosinski Brehm was born in Cleveland, Ohio, of Polish immigrant parents right before the Depression. After moving to Portland in 1965, she enjoyed a 21-year career as supervisor of volunteer literacy and English as Second Language tutors. Dorothy loves to proofread and to associate with writers.

"Spa-ghet"

GROWING UP IN CHICAGO during the fifties in our "Little Italy" neighborhood on the city's West Side, my family and neighbors could boast one indisputable claim to fame — the best pasta anyone could eat. We lived on the second floor of a five-story walk-up, and the smells that I remember emanating from the kitchens of each apartment were as distinctive as road signs. I could discern the scent of my mother's tomato sauce even with a head cold. My grandfather lived with us, and his recipe, which called for a little more "dago red" as he called it, was distinguished with a sweet, thick odor from the vino, onions, and fresh garlic. Down the hall I could smell Aunt Theresa's "spa-ghet" as she called it. From upstairs, Uncle John's ravioli wafted down into our apartment, and downstairs, in the little storefront where my uncles sold and repaired accordions, my Uncle Hank had a bottomless of pot of mustaccoli sauce brewing.

Which is all a way of saying that I have a primo collection of tips and advice from pasta aficionados to share with you.

Primo Pasta Sauce Tips

Blend your FRESH TOMATOES, or canned whole tomatoes, in a blender or food processor with at least 12 OUNCES OF TOMATO SAUCE and NEARLY EQUAL PARTS OF TOMATO PASTE for body. Before blending, add seasonings, such as FRESH OREGANO, PARSLEY, BASIL, ITALIAN SEASONING, and other HERBS. If you don't have good fresh GARLIC, what's a-matter, get some! Just kidding, that was one of my uncles speaking. You can substitute garlic powder or garlic salt in measured amounts. Remember, your sauce will get stronger as it simmers, so start conservatively.

If you do have fresh garlic, chop it and sauté it if you like, with MILD, SWEET, OR HOT ITALIAN SAUSAGES. Drain, chop, and dump into the sauce.

Chop a FEW GOOD SIZED ONIONS, and take a portion, perhaps ⅕ of them, and burn them. You can use a little OLIVE OIL in the frying pan if you like, so you don't ruin the pan, but the onions must be scorched and black. Drain and drop them in. The burnt onions negate the acidity of the tomatoes. If you don't burn the onions, try adding A LITTLE SUGAR OR WINE for the same effect.

After the sauce has blended thoroughly start adding other meats and ingredients. Depending on the size and amount you will have to add water to thin the sauce sufficiently. Try adding lean hamburger, sliced beef, meatballs, chicken or turkey parts, peppers, or mushrooms. Brew on low for 3-4 hours if possible. Keep a hunk of Italian bread by the stove so you can sample your sauce properly, twice an hour. Smack your lips, kiss your fingertips, and say "Mama mia, now THAT'S a spe'cy spa-ghet!"

———————◆———————

Rob Winike is secretary of the Oregon Writers Colony board. He lives in Portland and writes a Colonygram column called "Keeping Tabs on Publisher's Weekly." Author of Excel, Using Macros, *he is currently seeking representation for a co-written novel,* Redemption of Wolves.

M.F.K. Fisher Taught Me

I USED TO SPEND TIME watching my grandmother cook, bake bread, make mayonnaise and brew the best coffee. I grew up with the smell of coffee long before I was allowed to taste it. Years later, cooking became my creative outlet. I began reading cookbooks and stories of people who cooked, which led me to acquire a book from a library for a very long time. It was a book by M.F.K. Fisher. At that point in my life, her writing about cooking essentially changed how I thought about cooking. It was — learn from the cook or kitchen that you enjoy eating from and if at all possible take lessons from them. So I did. I worked at a Mexican restaurant, took Chinese cooking lessons, baked with the Finns and cooked with the Hungarians. My cooking improved and my knowledge of food grew. On one of my trips to the bookstore, I discovered that M.F.K. Fisher was back in print. I bought the collection of her books and returned my long overdue books to the local library.

The recipe I give to the Oregon Writers Colony is one that a dear friend of mine, who also had read M.F.K. Fisher, made and to which I have added other ingredients. We often talked of M.F.K. Fisher and her writing as if we knew her well.

Green Chili Soup

OLIVE OIL
2 TABLESPOONS CHOPPED PARSLEY
1/2-1 TEASPOON CUMIN
1 CLOVE GARLIC, CHOPPED
1 SHALLOT CUT UP OR 1/4 OF AN ONION, CHOPPED
2 STALKS CELERY, CHOPPED FINE
1/4 POUND MUSHROOMS, CHOPPED FINE
1-2 CANS GREEN CHILIES CANNED, CHOPPED
48 OUNCES CHICKEN BROTH
*1/2-1 POUND CHICKEN, TURKEY OR PORK CUT IN SMALL PIECES (IT CAN BE LEFT
     OVER OR FRESH)*
2-3 ZUCCHINI, GREEN OR A COMBINATION OF GREEN AND YELLOW
1 PACKAGE FROZEN CORN
SALT AND PEPPER TO TASTE

Begin by heating olive oil, add garlic, onion or shallots, and celery. If meat has not been cooked, add and brown slightly. Add

1 can of green chilies, cumin, parsley and mushrooms. Cook for a few minutes. Add broth and bring to a boil. Add vegetables. Bring to a boil and simmer for at least 15 minutes. Add salt and another can of green chilies if so desired and simmer up to an hour. Serve with flour or corn tortillas.

———————◆———————

Jennifer McCord, president of the Pacific Northwest Writers Conference board, has worked in the many areas of the publishing field for more than 15 years, including video and audio as well as books and marketing. Now she runs her own publishing consultant business to national and regional publishers.

Birthdays and Custard Pie

THE INVITATION READ LIKE THIS:
"Dear Friends,
"You are invited to my 60th birthday party.
"Where: Colonyhouse, Rockaway Beach, Oregon
"When: February 14, 1998
"For 22 years I was out of town on business on my birthday, either in New York or in Las Vegas at trade shows. Fifteen years ago I stopped in Denver to see my Uncle Mike on the way home from New York and arrived the night before my birthday in the middle of a snow storm. He picked me up at the airport and talked of buying me a special birthday dinner. After two weeks of working 10-hour days and eating rich New York restaurant food I begged him to just let me sleep in and then make me some of his good chili and instead of a birthday cake, a homemade custard pie. Uncle Mike, a retired baker, woke me up the next morning and served me custard pie for breakfast. The chili cooked all day while we visited, my uncle's infectious laugh made me forget the hectic New York schedule. Then the birthday dinner that night, home-made chili and custard pie. Every birthday since I've longed for another such feast.

"Uncle Mike is gone now, but in his honor and to satisfy my birthday cravings, Spud has agreed to make all of us chili and custard pie. It will make my birthday perfect if you come to the coast and share the meal. Join us at the Colonyhouse on Saturday, February 14, 1998. Arrive anytime after 10:00 a.m. and stay as late as you like. We can't offer you beds, but if you get a motel nearby we'll be glad to serve you breakfast on Sunday morning.

"Absolutely no presents. — *Marlene*"

My husband Spud and I arrived at the Colonyhouse Friday about two o'clock. He immediately began cooking and about eight that evening he put the finishing touches on six gallons of chili, four custard pies and 10 cups of custard. For dinner that night we baked two potatoes and stole a little bit out of the chili pot to top them off.

February 14 was a genuine Oregon coast soggy Saturday. It had rained all night and the puddles down by the front gate were six inches deep. But with all the lights turned on and a cheery fire going, the mellow old logs shone a welcome as the guests arrived. Sue Bronson and Linda Leslie were the first to arrive at 10:30.

Spud, the consummate cook, began putting out snacks. Cheese, crackers, veggies and his home-canned pickled asparagus. By noon when we began serving the chili, 18 friends had arrived. We ate, chatted, and the braver, more ambitious took drenching hikes on the beach.

As some guests left, others arrived. Early in the afternoon the party became a mini-Oregon Writers Colony reunion. Margaret Borland, the organization's first treasurer, Sharon Wood, the Colonygram's first editor, and Florence Samuel and Irene Emmert, early board members, reminisced about the early conferences and workshops. All in all, 28 friends came to share the occasion and the party didn't end until 12:30 a.m. Sunday morning when I reluctantly said good-by to Ray and Jean Auel.

I turned 60 two days later, still buoyed by the memories. Cards and flowers continued to arrive for almost a week as the friends who hadn't made it to the beach sent greetings. This decade got off to a great start for me.

Spud's recipe for chili is mentioned elsewhere in this book by Doreen Gandy Wiley, but here is the pickled asparagus recipe that everyone at the party requested.

Pickled Asparagus

18 POUNDS ASPARAGUS
4 QUARTS WHITE VINEGAR
4 QUARTS WATER
20 TABLESPOONS PICKLING SALT
2 TABLESPOON PICKLING SPICE (REMOVE THE CLOVES)
4 TABLESPOONS DILL SEED

Blanch the asparagus for 2 minutes and put into an ice water bath to stop cooking action and crisp the asparagus. Bring the water, vinegar and salt to a boil. Place spices into a cheese cloth bag and put into the boiling water. Keep water hot and let steep.

Drain asparagus on paper towels. Pack into hot sterilized jars, add a clove of garlic to each jar and cover with the hot mixture. Seal jars in a hot water bath canner. Pints for 10 minutes and quarts for 15 minutes.

Can be made without canning. Place in a jar or non-metallic container and let cool. Keep under refrigeration. Will keep for several weeks.

For variety add one or two, depending on taste, dried red peppers to each jar.

Ready to eat in 24 hours but gets better with age.

————◆————

Marlene Howard is cofounder of Oregon Writers Colony and current board member. She is partner in Media Weavers publishers. She is on the Pacific Northwest Writers Conference board and the University of Washington's Educational Outreach Writers' Program advisory board.

Like a Guadalajaran Gourmet

I GREW UP ON the outskirts of Phoenix, in a family where money was short and ran by so quickly that we rarely saw it. Our house was small and old, meals balanced but cheap. Every week we had beans for dinner. On a scale of disgusting to delicious, beans were the worst! Green chili, a rare treat, was off the scale high.

The summer I was eleven, Dad came home one afternoon with a bag of groceries and announced that he was making green chili. We were chased from the kitchen, to stand in the doorway, giddy with anticipation. Blonde heads sunburned to straw, skinny legs sticking out of sawed-off shorts, and freckled noses peeling like lizards, we watched Dad select the largest pot in the house. "We'll have plenty of leftovers," he said. I imagined a whole week of green chili and not one bean. It couldn't have been better if he'd said we would have Orange Crush and ice cream every night.

Though Scotch-Irish, Dad could talk and cook like a Mexican. With his black hair and dark skin it didn't take much imagination to see a Guadalajaran gourmet in our kitchen. (Mom was his Viking assistant.)

Cooking chili is slow-going and eventually we drifted away, bored, but checking every few minutes, "Is it done yet?"

Within an hour, the bubbling mixture began wafting invitations over the valley. Guests began arriving. Friends. Relatives. Neighbors. People we hadn't seen in years. Of course, they were all asked to dinner.

With each new arrival, my heart sank lower. That huge pot looked smaller and smaller. My dream of a beanless week would be eaten up before my very eyes. Mom discovered more cheese and lettuce to chop and dispatched me down the street to the Chinese store for more tortillas and milk.

By the time I returned, the house was filled beyond capacity. Men congregated in the kitchen, leaning on the walls, laughing around the stove. Women lounged in the living room, filling it with chatter and the tinkling of ice in tea glasses. The children played outside.

I knew there couldn't possibly be enough chili in Dad's tiny pot to feed that multitude! But, no time to worry! Outside were kids of all ages and no shortage of games to play. Every so often,

though, the smells drifting through the open kitchen window dragged me into the house for a progress report.

On one visit, Dad had me poll the company. "Hot or mild?" I asked them and reported the numbers. Then I watched as he found another pot and divided the chili, adding the secret ingredient to the "hot."

Finally dinner was served. The line began at the stove and wound through the kitchen doorway and around the living room. Dad stood at the stove, making the burros to order: mild or hot with just the right amounts of cheese. He rolled them himself, the "correct" way; fold bottom, fold one side, roll once, fold top, and roll again. Then he covered the top with more sauce and cheese. Mom stood at the table, garnishing with lettuce and pouring glasses of milk or tea.

My siblings and I, determined not to be "gringos" in front of company, chose the "hot." Dad smiled and added extra cheese. Mom doubled the lettuce.

Previous experimentation had shown us that milk sipped slowly, held in one's mouth even, quenched the fire, while gulping water fanned the flames. And SIPPING was macho!

The crowd filed into the living room, plates heaping and glassed brimming, to sit on the couch, chairs, kitchen chairs, lawn chairs, couch arms, chair arms, and the floor. Our plates rested on coffee tables, TV trays, and laps. After a round of compliments, everyone tried to eat before the swamp cooler petrified their tortillas.

The burros torched my lips and lit a line of fire from outside to in. We three exchanged teary smiles, nonchalantly sipping milk.

Somewhere between seconds and thirds, the "mild" ran out. No problem! Dad just served the "gringos" half the hot with twice the trimmings. The "hot" held out to the end, but my dream week of feasting was gone for good. No matter. At some point, amid groans and more compliments, guitars came out and took our fiesta into the night.

Green Chili Burros

2 POUNDS GROUND OR SHREDDED BEEF
1 1/2 TEASPOONS GARLIC POWDER
8 4-OUNCE CANS DICED GREEN CHILI
1 1/2 TEASPOONS CUMIN SEEDS
6 TOMATOES (PEELED AND DICED)
1 TEASPOON OREGANO
1 LARGE ONION (DICED)
1/2 TEASPOON PEPPER
PINCH OF CORIANDER
SALT TO TASTE

Brown meat. Place all ingredients in a pot. Cover with water. Boil until ingredients are soft and most of the water has boiled off. Thicken with flour. Roll in a flour tortilla with grated cheese.

(Secret ingredient: add DICED JALAPEÑOS. See story.)

———————

J. B. Allphin left Big City, Arizona, for Small Town, Oregon. She hopes someday to make the move from her day job to the writing life.

The LoHi Option
(aka Egg Burrito)

———◆———

THIS IS A BRUNCH ITEM. I usually cook one at a time, but it probably wouldn't be difficult to make two. I'm not sure about more. The question with the LoHi Option is how healthily virtuous you want to be. You can make it low in evil cholesterol and calories or hedonistically high.

EGG (OR VIRTUOUS ERSATZ EGG)
SLICED OR DICED ONION — RED, WHITE, YELLOW OR GREEN. WHATEVER.
LETTUCE, PLAIN OR FANCY
SPROUTS (I PREFER RADISH SPROUTS, BUT IF YOU WANT TO TRY THEM, YOU'LL
*   PROBABLY HAVE TO GROW YOUR OWN.)*
MEDIUM-SIZE FLOUR TORTILLA (TRY A GOOD, THICKER VARIETY)
SHREDDED CHEESE (SINFUL AGED CHEDDAR OR VIRTUOUS MOZZARELLA)
SALSA

Use your favorite small skillet, preferably the old grungy iron one, on medium or medium high heat. Melt a little butter in the skillet (or a little virtuous margarine, or spray with totally virtuous Pam). Break the egg (if you opt for sin) into a bowl and stir furiously with a fork. Next, throw enough onions in the skillet to cover the bottom in a lacy pattern.

While the onion is cooking, zap the tortilla in the microwave for twenty seconds on high power. Butter the tortilla, if you feel hedonistic, or margarine it, or eat it virtuously virgin.

Pour the stirred (or ersatz) egg over the onion, tipping the skillet to fill all the little holes in the lace. Then scatter the shredded cheese on top. Immediately turn off the heat and put on a tight lid. (But leave the skillet on the burner.)

Next, lay a few pieces of lettuce in the middle of the tortilla. Remember, you have to leave enough naked tortilla at the bottom and sides so you can fold the thing up.

Check the egg/onion/cheese stuff to see if the cheese is melted. If so, spread a wad of sprouts on half of it, then fold the other half over it. (And/or sprinkle on some sweet basil or fresh, chopped chives or parsley or salt and pepper or whatever sounds good.) It's ready to apply to the tortilla now, but there'll probably be too much, so use your spatula to trim out a piece that will fit nicely atop the lettuce. Fold up the tortilla. You'll need a toothpick to hold it together. Serve the extra egg stuff on the side or share it with a friend — Rover or Tinkerbell or whoever. Keep the salsa handy as you eat the LoHi Option and spoon on to taste.

I like to complement the LoHi Option with cucumber sliced about $1/8$" thick, lightly salted, and dolloped with salsa. Which is about as virtuous as you can get.

———————

M.K. Wren, who lives in Road's End, Oregon, wrote the acclaimed novel, A Gift Upon the Shore. *She also created the Conan Flagg mystery series, which debuted with* Curiosity Didn't Kill the Cat. *M.K. is a favorite workshop instructor for Oregon Writers Colony.*

Not Cholesterol-ically Correct

I'M NOT MUCH OF A COOK. My idea of a good dinner is a baked potato and cottage cheese. Toast and stewed tomatoes. Peanut butter on a slab of Swiss cheese.

A friend once opened my refrigerator to find 12 heads of cabbage and a grapefruit inside. Didn't seem a bit odd to me.

So this recipe isn't something I make very often. It's not microwaveable, for one thing. It also calls for a mixing bowl, knife, whisk, measuring cups and spoons and one of those 9x13" baking pans that's always jammed at the back of your cupboard, under a dusty pile of pans and jars and behind Aunt Dixie's mega 40-pound rotary mixer. Not something you want to pull out of your cupboard very often.

The recipe is not cholesterol-ically correct, either. Ham, cheese, eggs, butter. Who needs 'em any more? But the result tastes wonderful.

Grandma Georgia's Ham & Cheese Casserole

CUBE: 3 CUPS HAM
        3 CUPS FRENCH BREAD
        1/2 POUND CHEESES
MIX: 3 TABLESPOONS FLOUR
        3 TABLESPOONS MELTED BUTTER
        1 TABLESPOON DRY MUSTARD
        1 TABLESPOON WORCESTERSHIRE SAUCE
BEAT: 4 EGGS
        3 CUPS MILK

Layer half the cubed ingredients in the bottom of a 9x13" baking pan. Dab with seasonings, and layer remaining cubed ingredients on top. Beat eggs and milk. Pour over ham and cheese. Chill at least four hours. Bake for one hour at 350°F.

Tip: The seasonings make a kind of paste that won't spread evenly. Never mind. The eggs and milk help mix it all up.

Martha Ragland used to be a pretty good cook. Her career peaked in 1959, when her homemade bread won a blue ribbon at the Klamath County 4-H Fair. Since then her cooking career has been undistinguished.

Mermaid Dreams

In 1983 I experienced profound grief after encountering the life-sized marble statue of Emperor Caesar Augustus at the Vatican Exhibit in San Francisco. The events which followed led me through an outrageous process of uncovering my tragic life as Julia, Augustus' only "beloved" child. The book in progress details the quest for healing and peace for Julia and Augustus in current time.

"Mermaid Dreams" is a glimpse of one evening in Italy on my journey of self-discovery. My traveling companion, Peg, had been Julia's traveling companion and handmaiden Phoebe, who was hanged when Julia was arrested and exiled on charges of sexual scandal.

I STOOD ON THE VERANDA watching the starry heavens turn on the axis of Capri. I inhaled the fragrance of jasmine and oranges that drifted up from the gardens of Augustus below our room. Nudged by the enchanted beauty of Moroccan-styled corridors, red-tiled rooftops, and the placement of high cliffs over an azure sea, my adulterous past-life memory reawakened.

Peg's playful warning echoed within me, "Ulysses managed to escape this island. You and I will be lucky if we can summon the courage to do likewise."

Capri had captivated me with its zest for life: Mario's fagioli and his offer of pleasures laced with crisp wine. But how long could it last?

We left the doors to the veranda open all night, proof that we were a million miles from home. We couldn't sleep like that on the Oregon coast in late October. Fog might roll into the house and turn the bedding as damp as sea foam in a slippery tide.

I would not be meeting Mario at Marina Piccolo tomorrow even though Julia whispered in my head, "Can't we but play a little while? What could it hurt?"

All night in dreams I swam in the iridescent waters of hidden blue grottos with the double-tailed mermaid of Capri — and Mario.

Mario's Fagioli al Forno (baked beans)

1 POUND DRIED WHITE BEANS
1 HANDFUL FRESH SAGE LEAVES
2-3 TABLESPOONS EXTRA VIRGIN OLIVE OIL
1 CLOVE CRUSHED GARLIC, MORE IF YOU LIKE
SALT AND PEPPER
1 TEASPOON OR LESS DRIED, CRUSHED HOT PEPPERS WITH SEEDS

Soak beans overnight in water; drain. Add sage, olive oil, garlic and dried peppers. Add water to cover. Cover pot, place in 300°F oven. When beans boil, reduce heat to 250°F and simmer gently about 3 hours or until most of the water is absorbed. Leave slightly soupy. Add salt and pepper and, if you like, small pieces of ham, prosciutto or tuna. Serves 4. BUON APPETITO!

Pomodoro al forno e spaghetti

(baked tomato spaghetti)

3 POUNDS FIRM-RIPE ROMA TOMATOES
6 CLOVES MINCED GARLIC
1/2 CUP CHOPPED PARSLEY
4 TABLESPOONS OLIVE OIL
SALT AND PEPPER
1 POUND DRY SPAGHETTI
2 TABLESPOONS BUTTER
BASIL, 1/2 CUP FRESH OR 2 TABLESPOONS DRY
PARMESAN CHEESE, IF DESIRED

Cut tomatoes in half lengthwise and set, cut side up, in 9x13" baking dish. Sprinkle with salt and pepper. Mix garlic, parsley, and 2 tablespoons olive oil; pat mixture over tomatoes. Drizzle 2 tablespoons oil over tomatoes. Bake in 400°F oven one hour or until browned on top. Bring 3 quarts water to boil. Add spaghetti and cook, uncovered, 9 minutes. Drain.

Place butter in warm serving bowl, add basil, cooked tomatoes and pan juices. Add pasta. Add parmesan cheese if desired. Gently mix. Serves 4-6. BUON APPETITO!

———————

Sandy Kretzschmar traded her pottery studio and Oregon coast art gallery to write the story of her past-life as one of Rome's most scandalous women. She revised these recipes from their original sources after rediscovering the sensuous appeal of the land, the people, and the food of Italy.

Very 1950s, My Dear

THE YOUNG JOURNALIST WAS PLEASED, this day, with her move to the Northwest. She had traded constant prairie winds for the gentle breezes now playing around her hat. Behind her chair on the flower-filled brick patio above the lake stood an elegant house; before her white sails dotted blue waters. Trees in late-spring splendor filtered the overhead sun, bringing a perfect mixture of light and shade to the scene below. Crystal gleamed, silver shone, the ladies were dressed to the nines, looking sweet and elegant as they sipped mimosas and chatted lightly across their linen-clad tables.

The brunch was as perfect as the day. Browned link sausages, creamy scrambled eggs, crunchy with fresh mushrooms, colored by fresh parsley, spiced with Worcestershire. The first of the year's rich, flavorful Pacific Northwest strawberries.

And silver platters of orange sticky-rolls, fresh from the oven.

Enchanted as the writer was, full of mimosas and goodwill, her observing self noted that truly remarkable numbers of the little orange buns were disappearing down those elegant throats. As the platters kept coming, the writer began to wonder how this miracle of continuous supply happened, and resolved to find out. ("An old family recipe," she surmised, "They won't tell me.")

Later she found the kitchen and caterer. The woman was motherly-plump, dressed in starched white, and modestly happy that a guest had sought her out. "Thank heavens," the young woman thought, "not a thin, scary person."

"The sticky orange rolls," she asked tentatively. "How did you . . . what did you . . . they kept coming so fast . . . we ate so many! Could you have kept them coming all day?"

"Of course. That's one of my best secrets," she said. "I'll tell it to you — but only if you promise not to go into the catering business!"

The journalist kept on writing, never once tempted to provide competition to any caterer anywhere. However, she did put the "secret" to use right away, then passed it down the generation-ladder and across her friend-network. The results have fed squads of incredibly hungry young men as well as occasional elegant brunch ladies. Her children, now grandchildren, love to help make these delicate bites of sweetness.

Note: Everything in this menu will wait while you drink mimosas and become nostalgic!

All-purpose Brunch Menu

MIMOSAS OR NOT
EQUAL PARTS CHILLED ORANGE JUICE AND CHAMPAGNE,

Or equal parts pineapple and grapefruit juice, mixed well and thoroughly chilled. Serve either one in cooled wine glasses.

LINK SAUSAGES (THANKS, BETSY)
3 POUNDS LINK SAUSAGES
2 SLICED ONIONS
SLICED UNPEELED TART APPLES
1 POUND BROWN SUGAR

Place sausages in Dutch oven or roaster. Spread with onions, apples to cover and brown sugar. Cover. Cook at 300°F for 2½ hours.

Skim fat and remove "debris" before serving. This originally was intended as an appetizer. As a brunch item with this menu it serves 15-20, or 30-40 doubled. (Double the meat without doubling anything else.) Can be made it the day before and reheated.

CREAMY SCRAMBLED EGGS
3 DOZEN EGGS
1½ CUPS HALF-AND-HALF
1-2 TABLESPOONS WORCESTERSHIRE SAUCE (OPTIONAL)
3 TEASPOONS SALT
PEPPER TO TASTE
¼ CUP BUTTER
SLICED FRESH MUSHROOMS (CHOOSE YOUR QUANTITY) (OPTIONAL)
3-6 CHOPPED LITTLE GREEN ONIONS (OPTIONAL)
2 CUPS MEDIUM THIN WHITE SAUCE (2 TABLESPOONS EACH BUTTER AND FLOUR
*   TO 1 CUP MILK) OR USE CANNED*
CHOPPED FRESH PARSLEY

Beat eggs lightly with cream, salt, pepper and Worcestershire. Melt butter in very large frying pan. Add mushrooms and onions, cooking lightly. Pour in egg mixture and cook slowly, stirring occasionally, until almost set. Fold in hot white sauce while eggs are still creamy. Keep hot in a very slow oven (200 °F) or place over hot water on top of the range. Better yet, cook in big electric skillet and turn to low to await serving. Sprinkle before serving with lots of chopped fresh parsley. This will serve 24.

STICKY ORANGE ROLLS

PACKAGES OF REFRIGERATOR BISCUITS. (BUY WHATEVER IS ON SALE. BUY LOTS.)
ORANGE JUICE
SUGAR CUBES

Place biscuits side by side in baking pan with edges.

Pour orange juice into shallow bowl. For each biscuit, dip a sugar cube into the orange juice, hold it briefly so it will absorb some juice, then push it lightly but firmly into the dough. Bake according to package directions or until rolls are nicely browned.

After holding eight jobs in 10 years in a high technology firm, Sally Petersen founded a writing-based business, making less money, and having more fun. She's also writing essays and a non-fiction book about starting one-person businesses. As a non-fiction writer, Sally helps represent a small-but-mighty minority on the Oregon Writers Colony board.

Liquid Nitrogen Grapefruit Sorbet

A BOUT THE CREATION OF THE RECIPE: In rural Wyoming, where this recipe originated, you have to learn how to make do with what's on hand. You can't just run to the grocery store for something you've forgotten; the store is liable to be (a) 30 miles away, and (b) closed when you get there.

We had gathered for dinner with some friends in Ranchester, a whistle-stop town in the foothills of the Bighorn mountains. One of the people there remarked that home-made ice cream would go well with the meal, but a quick inventory revealed that we didn't have all the ingredients for ice cream, nor did we have enough ice.

What we did have, however, was grapefruit juice, honey, and a lot of liquid nitrogen. Liquid nitrogen? Just happened to have that lying around, eh? Well, yes, actually. One of the friends we were

dining with was a veterinarian, and he used it for cold-branding horses. Much more humane than hot-branding, and you never know when you'll need to brand a horse.

Well, sorbet is just sweetened, frozen juice, and one of the other dinner guests knew what proportions of juice and honey to use, so we decided to give it a try. At first we thought about using the liquid nitrogen in place of ice in a regular ice-cream maker, but we were afraid of what it would do to the plastic parts. After all, plastic breaks easily enough when it's merely cold; when it's superchilled it's fragile as glass.

Then we thought about pouring it directly into the batter.

Nitrogen is all around us in the air, after all; there's nothing toxic about it.

So after some discussion of which ingredient to pour into the other (Is it acid into water, or water into acid? None of us could remember, or determine what relevance it had to nitrogen), we decided upon the following procedure, and it worked first time.

Afterward we had fun freezing marshmallow chicks and blowing them up in the microwave. When something goes from -300°F to +200°F or so, it expands an *amazing* amount. We laughed until our sides hurt.

Nitrogen narcosis, or just weird friends? Hard to tell.

Liquid Nitrogen Grapefruit Sorbet

4 PARTS GRAPEFRUIT JUICE
1 PART HONEY
4-8 PARTS LIQUID NITROGEN (AVAILABLE FROM OXYGEN OR WELDING SUPPLY STORES)

Dissolve honey in grapefruit juice. (Heating will help if it's stubborn.) Using metal pan or shatterproof bowl and a wooden spoon, stir mixture while pouring nitrogen directly into it. Be careful! It will spatter at first. Pour slowly and keep stirring to help aerate freezing mixture. It will look like the witches' cauldron from MacBeth — this is normal. Stop stirring when mixture freezes solid. Allow excess nitrogen to boil off before tasting! Sorbet is ready to eat when it starts to soften again.

Some tips for handling liquid nitrogen: Wear gloves, a coat, and eye protection. Never touch liquid nitrogen directly, or allow it to contact bare skin.

Store nitrogen in thermos bottles, but do not tighten caps or excess pressure will build up. Pre-chilling grapefruit/honey mixture will help conserve nitrogen. Leftover nitrogen is good for freezing and shattering common household objects. Keep a responsible adult nearby at all times; it will drive them crazy.

———————

Jerry Oltion has been a gardener, stone mason, carpenter, oilfield worker, forester, land surveyor, rock 'n' roll deejay, printer, proofreader, computer consultant, movie extra, and garbage truck driver. For the last 15 years, he has also been a writer. He even cooks a little in his spare time.

Summer Infusion

M Y SISTER, PEG, SURFS the Internet. A lot. So it was no
surprise when the e-mail arrived telling me of this wonderful vacation she had found on the Internet. "It's a new place at
Disney World called The Disney Institute. We would be at the
cutting edge of things as it doesn't even open until February! How
does a July vacation sound?" I read the message but did not have
time to respond.

The new e-mail read, "Did you get my e-mail? Doesn't it sound
exciting? I'm faxing you some information to get you enthused."
My response was short. "It sounds interesting; but you want me to
go to FLORIDA in JULY with all that HEAT and HUMIDITY?"

Peg persisted. Next she mailed me a brochure, video and a
schedule of classes. I was beginning to wear down. Again on the
phone, "Did you get the package? It is soooo cool! We could learn
from all these top notch professionals and have fun doing it. We
could all take things that appealed to each of us and share. Don't
tell me this doesn't interest you!"

Persistence and technology paid off and she won me over. Class
schedules in hand, Peg, her husband, Guy, and her son, Josh,
departed from Alaska and I from Oregon to rendezvous at The
Disney Institute in Florida.

I was not prepared for what I encountered. I expected the
crowds and noise I had experienced in the Magic Kingdom, not
this tranquil setting. Guests stayed in bungalows or townhouses
separated by lush landscaping. The person who checked me in
also helped me get settled into our bungalow. When I tried to tip
her she said, "I can't accept that, this is all part of your package.
Enjoy your stay." I'm sure the surprised expression was still on my
face as she drove off in her golf cart.

The bungalow had a living area, mini-kitchen, bedroom and
bath. A patio overlooked a lake where ducks glided and blue
herons and snowy egrets graced the shores. After unpacking I
picked up my golf cart. Most guests were walking or using golf
carts to get from place to place; very few cars were seen. Since I
normally drive with hand controls, I took the cart for a drive
around the complex to get used to the pedals on the floor. It was
good there were not too many people as I jerked and stopped my
way around! The second trip was much smoother and I began to

enjoy the peacefulness and beauty. I was relaxing already. Peg and her family arrived about midnight and we settled in; we would begin our classes early the next morning.

After a quick breakfast we went our separate ways for our first classes. In only two hours Peg made a delicious peach pie and we all ate samples; Josh and Guy created a short clay animation film, and I brought home a portable herb garden. We learned tips that made things easier. We learned from the best in their fields; they provided everything for the classes, and we ate or took home anything we made. I was glad I decided to do a "sampler," taking classes in gardening, animation, design art and culinary. Some of the others tried broadcasting, architectural design, acting and make-up, or the youth programs. Peg even managed to squeeze in a foot massage at the spa.

All the classes were informative and fun but it was the culinary classes that drew the family together. It was amazing when any one of us was taking a culinary class the rest of the family materialized just as the cooks were coming out of the kitchen to taste the goodies. One time Peg and I had just sat down to eat. Both Josh and Guy were in other classes so the food was ours alone. I looked up to see that Guy had skillfully incorporated his "Making Better Videos" class with our sampling by videotaping our food just before he sat down and picked up a fork!

As I look back on this vacation, I realized that while having a good time we learned we could do things that always before had seemed too complicated. Here are a few recipes that I found pretty easy but that will let you wow your friends and family.

Baked Brie in Phyllo Dough with Black Sesame Seeds

2 OUNCES BRIE CHEESE
2 PHYLLO DOUGH FROZEN SHEETS
1 TABLESPOON BLACK SESAME SEEDS
1 OUNCE OLIVE OIL

Cut Brie half into four triangles. Stick together two pieces to form a rectangle. Brush olive oil on phyllo sheets. Place the Brie on the phyllo and roll up. Preheat oven to 350°F. Brush olive oil on all exposed surfaces. Sprinkle the top surface with black sesame seeds. Place on parchment paper and cook for 5-10 minutes or until golden brown. Serves 2.

Lemon Basil Granita (fruit ice)

2 CUPS SUGAR
2 CUPS WATER, HOT
1 TABLESPOON LEMON ZEST
1 CUP LEMON JUICE
3/4 CUP FRESH BASIL, CHOPPED
7 CUPS WATER

Prepare the syrup by adding sugar to the hot water and stirring until dissolved. Then add lemon zest. Let cool. Add remaining ingredients and place in freezer in a 9x13" pan. Allow the mixture to freeze for one hour and then scrape ice crystals that form around the edge into the center. Continue to scrape every 45 minutes until slush forms. Store in smaller air tight containers. 20 servings. SUGGESTION: The syrup can be made adding the lemon zest and juice and stored in the refrigerator as a concentrate. Mix the concentrate with sparkling water (1:7 ratio) for a refreshing beverage in the summer.

Summer Fruit Infusion

4 CUPS CHARDONNAY WINE
2 CUPS SWEET DESSERT WINE
1/2 CUP ORANGE JUICE
1/2 CUP SUGAR
1 PINT FRESH BLUEBERRIES
1 PINT FRESH STRAWBERRIES, SLICED
1/2 PINT FRESH RASPBERRIES
1/4 CUP FRESH MINT, CHOPPED
FRESH MINT SPRIGS, FOR GARNISH

Bring 1 cup of Chardonnay to a simmer and place half of the chopped mint in the wine. Let it steep for 15 minutes. Strain and discard mint. Add the rest of the ingredients 1 hour before serving. Garnish with fresh mint. Serve with sugar cookies. 12 servings.

Kitty Purser, a native Oregonian, has traveled extensively discovering new and exciting places and the cultures that flourish there. She is a supporter of the Americans With Disabilities Act and has written about persons with disabilities for newsletters and magazines.

For Love, Not Duty

TO ME, A HOME IS NOT A HOME WITHOUT BOOKS all over the place and something delicious simmering in the kitchen. I have always thought that the preparation of food for family and friends is a gesture of love, not duty.

Some of my happiest times have been spent writing and cooking, one activity in harmony with the other. As a stew bubbles or a casserole sends out its savory odors, the characters form, the words crowd, struggling to spring full-paragraph from my brain.

I started writing as a child, hugging my words to myself in the way of an only child, scared to let anybody else read what I wrote for fear they'd think I was peculiar. I realize now that I was in awe of myself, if that's possible. I wondered: *Where do all these words come from?* I still wonder.

Usually my writing was going on while Mother was cooking. And what a cook she was! The house was filled with the smell of baking powder biscuits, stuffed green peppers, roasting young chickens, fresh apricot pie, lemon meringue pie and everything prepared "from scratch," of course.

I remember weekly trips to a place that no longer exists, the old Farmer's Market in downtown Portland, several blocks redolent with fresh vegetables and fruits in their seasons, fresh sea food of all kinds, poultry, cheeses by the wheel or by the slice, freshly baked breads and pastries.

I remember Mother wanting to "feel" the tomatoes to make sure they were ripe, and being yelled at by the stall keeper to "not touch the produce." (A far cry from today's supermarkets where everyone touches everything, including tomatoes so hard you could break your toe if you dropped one.)

On very special Saturday nights my father would whip up a cake, two layers, with frosting. I was in charge of making the frosting, carefully watching the boiling sugar and water until it spun a thin thread, 6 to 8" long, when dropped from the tip of a spoon.

Part of this job was the right to lick the beaters and bowl after the frosting had been spread on the cake. Then Mother and Dad and I would eat cake and read the early edition of the Sunday Oregonian before I went happily to bed, feeling safe and loved and protected.

In the freshness of marriage I remember eating succulent Alaska crab legs in a light cheese sauce sprinkled with paprika at a wonderful old seafood restaurant with white-jacketed waiters and linen tablecloths. My husband and I would talk over all the exciting events of the work day, then hurry home to snuggle and admire each other extravagantly, as lovers do.

I remember covering the national convention of the International Bakers Association the year the president of General Mills announced a startling new product: their first cake mix. He mentioned that his company could have made the product so that it only required adding milk, but that since women aren't happy unless they feel they have prepared a dish, the mix required adding a couple of eggs besides the milk.

At that same convention, the mayor of Portland, Dorothy McCullough Lee, walked onto the platform to deliver her speech to the group, parking her shopping bag, from which soared a bunch of celery, against the podium. Mrs. Jackson, president of the board of directors of the "Oregon Journal," always referred to this mayor as "Mrs. Airwick."

When the children were all at home and I was working 14 hours a day running an advertising agency, I made a point of spending my weekends in orgies of cooking and baking, with everything going into the freezer for subsequent thawing.

In those days the recipes were more involved than they are today. There was a recipe in one of the women's magazines that involved carefully spreading a leg of lamb with a mixture of blackberry jam, mustard and sour cream, then slowly roasting. It sounds horrible but it was actually delicious. I've never been able to find that recipe since.

What a riotous place the kitchen was then! Kids and their friends sneaking quietly in when my back was turned to abscond with small chunks of top round steak, browned and crisp, ready for immersing in beef broth with wine, vegetables and whole garlic cloves. Lots of garlic.

I've never been a "crowd cooker," one who wants friends in the kitchen while meal preparation is going on. I like to hear the music of people in the house, but in the kitchen with me? No, because when I cook I totally concentrate on preparing the meal, just as when I write I totally concentrate on what I'm writing.

When I got rid of the advertising agency and began to seriously write, Joe and I lived on a houseboat where the kitchen, living room, and one bedroom were on the second floor. I set up my office under an east window right outside the kitchen, and soon was adjusting seasonings while I thought about how to create suspense, how to lure a reader into the story, how to bring the story to a satisfying conclusion.

I prefer recipes that in themselves are not too time-consuming in preparation but take a long time to cook, thus filling the house with mouth-watering smells.

I don't cook nearly as much anymore. For one thing, I am writing full time. Now there are usually only the two of us and since Joe has had a stroke and is diabetic, I have to be very selective about what he eats.

But I remember with a loving feeling the special foods and get-togethers of the past. My youngest son, Matt, is now the superb cook of the family, specializing in game, steelhead, and Chinook salmon. He, like his mother, cooks with love for those he loves.

And my darling daughter Meg, now the mother of three girls herself, once in a while will call and ask, "Mom, would you make some Indian pudding?"

When I hear that I know that maybe she's a little blue, or too tired, and my heart leaps because I know that once again I can provide love and comfort for my young.

———————————

Naomi M. Stokes is the New York Times bestselling author of the widely acclaimed nonfiction book, The Castrated Woman. *She also is the author of* The Tree People, *a novel set on the Quinault Indian Reservation in Washington State. Her second novel is* The Listening Ones. *A former reporter, Stokes is part Cherokee and a third-generation Oregonian. She lives in Hillsboro, Oregon.*

Of Philosophy and Laundry

Dear James,   June 3, 1996

ONE WEEK FROM TODAY you'll be graduating from high
school . . . eight days from now you'll be moving out on your
own. I hope you'll read this letter, but should you get no further
than this sentence, I want to say again that I love you, that I
understand why you need to go, and that I have confidence in your
ability to succeed.

There seem to have been many words shouted lately with little
communication. For the part I've played in losing my temper and
judging your choices, I'm sorry. I hope that when you leave here
you will take with you the attributes of honesty, integrity, personal
responsibility, honor, and pride in a job well done. The words may
sound like old-fashioned gibberish, nevertheless, they are the
qualities that transform a student into a professional, a youth into
a man. Listen if you will to just a little more advice from your
mother, who's had to be bound, gagged, and dragged kicking
through every life lesson . . . .

Recognize the difference between what you want and what you
need and set your goals accordingly, my love. See them through,
especially when it comes to accomplishing what you need. Pay the
price for what you want, be willing to compromise when you must,
but think before you act and make decisions that will bring you
enduring happiness.

Be creative and kind, a single thought can change your life, a
single act can change your world.

Stand by your passions, be not afraid to outgrow them. Change
is natural, embrace it as an adventure! Whatever path you choose,
walk it with opened eyes, heart, and mind and you will experience
the joy of others as well as the chance to evaluate your beliefs.

With faith and a sense of humor as your best friends, you will
never be lonely. Make time to honor your spiritual foundations
and to laugh every day. Neither faith nor humor is tangible, yet in
this world of materialistic objectives, they are the most elusive of
treasures, even love is abundant by comparison.

Above all cherish freedom. Freedom is not living alone or
without obstacles, but the choice of a wise man to know the fears

and desires of his soul — to confront each honestly, to find resolution, to live in harmony, and to know peace.

On a less philosophical note, you're always welcome to bring your laundry by. I'm including my recipe for fried rice, I know it's one of your favorites (it's also healthy, inexpensive and can be made in "kegger" quantities). Do you remember that when you were a little boy you hated rice, said it was bird tongues? But then, you used to love broccoli, called it "trees," now you wouldn't touch it with anything shorter than a cattle prod. Change . . . but I digress.

Fried Rice (aka Bird Tongues, Bouillon, and Whatever's Not Growing Fuzz in the Fridge)

2 TABLESPOONS COOKING OIL
1 CHOPPED ONION
1 CUP CHOPPED VEGETABLES (FROZEN WILL DO)
6 CUPS OF COOKED RICE (BROWN OR WHITE)
1 TABLESPOON SESAME OIL
1 TEASPOON CHINESE FIVE SPICE (OR MIX YOUR OWN WITH CINNAMON, STAR ANISE, CLOVES, GINGER, FENNEL)
*1 LARGE TEASPOON OF POWDERED CHICKEN BOUILLON (IF YOU USE CUBES, **REMOVE FOIL** AND BREAK UP WELL IN A TABLESPOON OF BOILING WATER)*
PEPPER AND SOY SAUCE (TO TASTE)
CHILI FLAKES
SALSA (OPTIONAL)

Burner on medium. Sauté onion until soft, add vegetables and stir until cooked. Add rice and mix well. Season with sesame oil, five spice, bouillon, pepper, soy sauce, and chili. Experiment — a dash of curry powder, minced garlic and ginger add an interesting flavor. Any kind of vegetables are good from bok choy to chestnuts (if you use canned, drain the water first).

Shrimp, diced chicken, beef — minced or strips, are a good touch. If the fish or meat is not already cooked, sauté it with your onion before adding vegetables. A fried egg on top was always one of my favorites, or add two eggs (already scrambled) after stirring in rice. Cashews, sesame seeds, even walnuts are tasty. I know you're not too crazy about tofu, but if you change your mind — stir fry 1-inch tofu cubes with garlic, onion, and butter in a separate pan and add the cubes to your fried rice just before serving.

Don't forget to brush, and as your Aunt Gaylin would say, "Floss only those teeth you wish to keep." We're here when you need us.

Love,
Mom

— *from life work in progress* Letters to My Sons and Daughters

---

Morgan Escalante is a retired broadcast journalist with 10 years of experience working in the Middle East and Southeast Asia. She now lives in Oregon with her husband and teenage children, Steinbeck the parrot, Maya the cat, and three goldfish —F. Scott, Zelda, and Gertrude. Between raising and writing, she practices Buddhism, teaches meditation, and assists others through past-life regression hypnosis. She's 39 years old.

Cooking Chinese Style

I t's snowing out there pretty good, so we should find some fresh tracks in the morning," Jones said as he began sipping his second cup of gin and lemonade. "The worst snow I ever saw here was in '51. Four of us came to camp that year. Your grandfather, Cecil Funmaker, Wilson Spino, and me. We took two big elk early, but then it dried up. With just three days left of the season, Red Shirt and Wilson left with the elk, but Cecil and I decided to see it through. So the day after they went up the old road to Halfway, it started to snow. And I mean snow — that day, all night, the next day and night. Forty inches, almost four feet. Cecil and I had to shovel a mountain of snow to uncover the woodpile. We had the old Willys pickup then, and it was just a hump in the snow."

"I've never seen that much snow," Jack said.

"I never want to again," Jones said. "But anything can happen in these mountains. Well, at first we weren't worried because we figured as how the road crews or forest rangers or somebody would come in after us, but they never did. The guys in the lower elk camps walked to farmhouses. But we was just stuck. There was wood and a little whiskey, but not much food.

"After a week, it got right lean. The whiskey was gone, and Cecil drank some liniment that made him half crazy. For three days we ate nothing but Violet Supreme."

"What's that?" Jack asked.

"Violet Supreme? Awfulest stuff ever. White rice and grape jelly — heated up. I still can't eat grape jelly without thinking of it. By that time I was too weak to cut wood, and Cecil just stayed in his sleeping bag and moaned. Finally, it got so cold in the tent that his false teeth froze to the glass.

"I about give up myself, and just crawled in my sleeping bag to freeze, figuring they could bury me in it. I closed my eyes and dreamed I was back on the reservation drinking whiskey with Red Shirt and Wilson . . . .

"Then, all of a sudden, the tent flap goes back and there's something white there-I figure maybe my angel-but it was Red Shirt all covered with snow from walking under pine branches. He had food and whiskey with him, and extra snowshoes so we could walk as far as the bridge at Indian Crossing."

"How'd he get there?" Jack asked.

Jones had another cupful of the lemonade and gin, favoring the gin this time. "Three's about right," he said. "He come by snowplow. Wilson's brother-in-law worked for county roads up around Baker. When Red Shirt and Wilson found out the highway crews wasn't going to plow thirty-five miles of switchback road from Halfway for two froze-ass Indians, they got Wilson's brother-in-law's keys and swiped a snowplow from the county yard. They damn near ruined it, too, learning how she worked, but they plowed the road from Halfway. It took three days. The bridge at Indian Crossing wouldn't hold a plow, so Red Shirt snowshoed the rest of the way.

"When he dumped his pack, he had six of the biggest steaks you ever saw — store-bought — none of your tough reservation beef. Red Shirt built up the fire good and started cooking those steaks. Then he saw the pan that still had some of the Violet Supreme in it. He stuck his finger into the rice and grape jam, tasted it, then smiled and said, 'Well, now. I see while you boys was up here you learned to cook Chinese style.'"

— from Winterkill, *1984, Dell Publishing*

Violet Supreme

WHITE RICE
BUTTER
GRAPE JELLY

Cook rice and add 1 tablespoon butter per quart. Add 1-2 cups grape jelly per quart, depending on your sweet tooth. Serve hot. Bottled hot pepper sauce or curry may be added, depending on what's left in camp.

Serve with Seagrams 7 and 7-Up or any other drinks available.

———◆———

Craig Lesley received several awards for Winterkill, *including the Pacific Northwest Booksellers Association award for best book of the year. He has followed* Winterkill, *with two more acclaimed novels,* River Song *and* The Sky Fisherman. *In 1986 Craig, a native Oregonian, received a National Endowment for the Arts fellowship.*

Throughout the years Oregon Writers Colony (OWC) has used various formats to bring writers together for short periods without charge. Readings have been held in members homes. Portland's main library has been used for afternoon readings, while "Literateas" were held for some time at Portland's elegant Heathman Hotel. Currently OWC offers a similar format — readings and writers discussing their craft — at Pick Me Up Tuesdays in a local bookstore.

Craig Lesley was among the first of the dozens of local and regional writers to read at the OWC Literary Salons which began in 1985. Several are represented in this volume.

Among the others who have read their work at salons, or taught workshops and classes for the Colony are Robin Cody, Voyage of a Summer Sun *and* Ricochet River; *John Daniel,* The Trail Home, *and* Looking After; *Molly Gloss,* The Jump-Off Creek; *and Phil Margolin,* Gone But Not Forgotten.

A Kitchen of One's Own

Or, the ABCs of Bachelorhood:
Mom's Advice for Real Food

———————

THE TIME COMES when "a room of one's own" isn't enough. It has to be "a place of one's own." I understand. But Mom is Mom is Mom, and I must tell you there is little joy — and even less real nourishment — in the fast food/fran food, pick up/take out world.

There's a place for you in the kitchen at your new place. Aprons are made for guys as well as gals, and "I can't cook!" is as silly as "I can't write!" Anyone can manage the basics. Get started, keep learning, and you'll be surprised at what you can turn out. Here are some starter ideas.

A Apples. Always keep a few on hand. Also, watch for artichokes in season. (To cook: trim top, part of stem; boil, covered, in 1" of water for 20-30 minutes.)

B Bananas (not beer). Or biscuits, as in refrigerated tubes; don't forget bagels.

C Candy, cookies, cake, chocolate. *No, no, no.* Instead, chicken breasts, broiled until no pink juices run out when poked; cook extra for sandwiches, salads, taco filling. Boneless, skinless pieces are fast, convenient: stir-fry with green peppers and onions to go with rice, or to make fajitas.

D Deli. Wafer-thin ham or roast beef and cheese on a good, crusty roll makes a great lunch.

E Eggs. Learn to boil, poach and scramble them. Two or three a week makes for good, cheap protein. (Soft-boiled: cover with 1" of water in saucepan; bring to boil, then simmer 3 minutes; hard-boiled: simmer 12-15 minutes. Drain, cover with cold water to cool quickly.)

F French fries under the broiler: scrub potatoes, cut into long wedges, coat with oil and sprinkle with salt. More F-words? French bread makes a fast, fresh pizza, and flour tortillas are super for cheese crisps, burritos.

G Ground beef + sauce + pasta is a fast, filling meal. Or, use it for the standard . . . .

H Hamburgers, of course.

I Ice cream. Yes, it's a staple.

J Juice or fresh fruit, every day.

K Kraut topped with a good sausage warms a cold winter's night. It's summer? Go for kabobs on the grill.

L Lasagna. Check the recipe on the package and pick up the rest of the ingredients while you're at the store. Don't forget lettuce.

M Milk. Again, every day. Mom's going to check on this.

N Noodles — or pasta if you're feeling sophisticated. Keep some on hand for a never-fail dinner-starter.

O Onions. Oatmeal. Often overlooked, but hearty and satisfying.

P Pasta's been covered. Another kitchen staple is potatoes, for those broiler fries or simply baked (about 1 hour at 375°F). Or peel, quarter and tuck them around a small beef roast, along with onion chunks.

Q Quick stuff: Nothing wrong with soup and a grilled cheese sandwich for lunch or supper.

R Rice: 1 cup regular long-grained rice, 2 cups cold water, sprinkle of salt in a saucepan. Bring to boil, stir, cover, cook on low heat, 15-20 minutes. Don't peek. Steam is the key.

S Sausage, grilled in a cast iron frying pan with onion and green pepper slices, along with some of that leftover rice. Don't eat this stuff every day, but once in a while — Mmmm.

T Tea, as in sun tea: 1 teabag in a quart jar of cool water; set it out on a sunny day. If you think that's too obvious, tell me why they sell cans of iced tea.

U Use by dates — on milk, meats: protein foods can grow nasty critters when left at room temperature. They may not smell spoiled but they can sure wreck your insides. The "24-hour flu" just might be food poisoning.

V Vegetables. Skip those greasy snacks. Instead, keep a bag of "rabbit food" in the fridge. Start with carrot and celery sticks and move on to cauliflower, broccoli. Trust me — raw veggies taste better than cooked.

W White bread vs. whole grain? Get whole grain.

X Checklist for kitchen staples: eggs, milk, cheese, rice, pasta and sauce, peanut butter, real butter or margarine, vegetable oil, cereal, soup.

Y Yogurt: 2 million Turks can't be wrong. Get a tub of plain — spice it up for a baked potato topping or veggie dip. Or sweeten lightly, mix in fruit.

Z Zucchini. OK, it's a stretch, but try it with tomatoes.

———————

With two sons off on their own, Myrna Daly left her job as editor and publications manager at Kansas State University and returned to the Portland area to launch a writing and editing business.

Season to Taste

Ada's son-in-law, Jeff, said he was going to make pesto for dinner with the fresh basil a friend had given him. "Yum," she said. "Can we come too?"

She added a laugh to make it easier for him to refuse, in case he didn't want her and Fred intruding.

"Sure," Jeff said. "We'll keep it casual. Pesto, fettucine, green salad, wine."

Ada liked his calm manner, so different from their first meeting, when he had tried frantically to impress them with his wit. She was sure that her daughter would be embarrassed by this tall, bristly young man, and they'd never see him again. But no, Sandy loved him, she wanted to marry him, and as Ada often said, she'd always been a sassy child with a mind of her own.

After the wedding, as it turned out, Jeff relaxed and Ada grew quite fond of him. He was crazy about Sandy and he was good to Travis, even though the six-year-old was Sandy's child, not his. That was enough to convince Ada. High time that boy had a man he could count on to be there.

"Fred and I will bring corn on the cob," she said. "We'll stop at the farmers' market, after our walk in the woods with Travis."

In the bird refuge north of town, the wind whipped their hair and sent clouds scudding over the oak trees. The air smelled crisp. Fred watched through the binoculars for sandhill cranes.

Travis pocketed acorns and kicked the crackling brown leaves, Ada gathered teazle and thorny branches strung with scarlet rose hips.

In the car, on the way home, Fred said, "I'm tired of pesto. We've had a lot of it lately."

Ada considered. "I guess I am too. I'll call Jeff and tell him maybe we'll bring something else."

She phoned. "We're pestoed out, Jeff. How about if we bring a chicken, already cooked?"

After a beat of silence, Jeff said, "I wish I'd known that. I already went to the store, and I'm fixing it now."

"Oh. Well, if we decide we definitely want chicken, we'll bring some. Don't worry about it."

She hung up the phone and was suddenly appalled at what she'd said. How could I have done that? How rude, how tactless. She squirmed. Her mother had taught her that being inconsiderate was the worst of all sins.

Later, bearing dried weeds, late corn, the last figs from their neighbor's tree, and a robust red wine, they drove to Jeff and Sandy's apartment. Ada wore oak leaves in her hair.

"You look like the autumn equinox in person," Sandy said. "Come on in, we're ready to throw the pasta in the pot."

Ada walked directly to Jeff, who was lighting the kindling in the fireplace. "I will not take off my jacket until you tell me I'm forgiven for inviting myself to dinner and then calling to tell you I don't want what you're serving," she said. "I can't believe I did that."

He laughed. "It did sound kind of strange. Did you bring chicken?"

"No, of course not. Pesto will be wonderful."

"Well, knowing how you felt, I found some CHORIZO SAUSAGE and thought I'd throw that in too. This won't be traditional, but I think it'll be good."

And it was good. TWO CUPS OF FRESH BASIL with 1/2 CUP SHELLED WALNUTS (pine nuts were too expensive, Sandy said), 1/3 CUP OF GOOD PARMESAN CHEESE, and 1/3 CUP OF EXTRA-VIRGIN OLIVE OIL ("How can you be extra-virgin," Fred asked, "any more than you can be extra-pregnant?" "*You* can't, but olive oil can," Ada answered) were mooshed together in the food processor, with the oil drizzled in a bit at a time until it all had the consistency of mayonnaise.

Jeff dropped in 1/2 TEASPOONFUL OF SALT and a PEELED CLOVE OF GARLIC. Then another clove. And another. And another. "My word," Ada marveled. "How much garlic do you use in this?"

"As much as it takes," he said with a grin, and Ada's last reservations about her daughter's choice in husbands faded away. He stopped at eight cloves and ground the mixture again. Then he put it into a mixing bowl and stirred in a 1/4 CUP OF CHOPPED, SAUTÉED RED BELL PEPPER, more for color and texture than flavor — what could compete with that garlic? — and scooped it into a big white bowl, a wedding gift from Ada and Fred. He mixed in the cooked PASTA, coating every *al dente* strand.

"Corn's ready," Sandy sang out. "Salad's ready. Pour the wine, Fred." She never called him Dad. No one expected her to, not when they knew how she revered the memory of her father. She and Fred were friends now, after a couple of stormy high school years — closer than she might have been with the hero-father, if he'd lived, Ada sometimes thought.

They lighted the candles and took their places at the table and toasted each other and autumn and abundant food, and ate it all.

"I love garlic," Travis said.

"A good thing, too," Ada said.

She looked around the table at the loved faces and felt a quick gratitude. Muzzy with wine, contentedly full, she raised her glass and said, "To small miracles."

The others looked at her quizzically. She didn't explain, so they shrugged, laughed, and drank to her toast. Ada plucked a fig from the basket on the table and took a bite of the sweet, luscious fruit.

———————

Marilyn McFarlane is a Portland writer. Her travel guides include Quick Escapes in the Pacific Northwest, Northwest Discoveries, *and, most recently, the fifth edition of* Best Places to Stay in the Pacific Northwest. *She also is the author of* Sacred Myths: Stories of World Religions, *a retelling of some of the best-known stories of seven spiritual traditions.*

Nothing Like a Man

I'M OLDER NOW, but as I remember my youth, there was nothing like a man. And the game, when you found him, was to somehow draw him into your life. If he didn't invite you out, the only recourse was to invite *him* to dinner at your place. Under these circumstances, even the least inspired, most indifferent cook in the world (a title to which I could lay as good a claim as any working girl) needed to produce a delicious meal. Not only that, if the dinner worked properly, there might be breakfast to fix in the morning!

So, I solved both of the problems outlined above, and I am about to lay on you one fool-proof pair of meals that will leave the most discriminating man convinced you know your way around the kitchen.

For dinner, serve beef Stroganoff from the *Fanny Farmer Cookbook*. It's deviously easy to cook. Use real beef filet, fresh mushrooms, real Hampshire sour cream. Quick-cooking rice is okay, if

you don't know how to cook rice. Add a nice fruit salad and some soft rolls; you won't even need dessert. This always worked for me — the dish has such a classy name — and it's *good!*

But what about the morning after? Are you going to destroy the illusion with rubbery scrambled eggs, soggy waffles, limp bacon, or cereal from a *box*? What non-cook can produce a good meal first thing in the morning?

Solution: Make breakfast ahead of time, when you are safely alone in the kitchen, and no one is looking over your shoulder. The following recipe makes a breakfast (add a banana, milk, and good coffee) that can be fixed at a moment's notice. It is loaded with protein and tastes wonderful.

You can even take this stuff along when you travel. If you feel like I do about going out in public before breakfast (and before brushing your teeth), a bag of "Morning Rescue" and a quart of milk in your traveler's ice chest lets you eat (and brush) in your motel room, before you face the world. It's great for a writer's week at Colonyhouse, as well.

I always keep a bag of my granola in the freezer. I haven't had a man in my life for a long time, but I'm ready, in case one turns up!

Morning Rescue Granola

Mix together in a large baking pan:

1 LARGE BOX (42 OUNCES) OLD FASHIONED ROLLED OATS
4 OUNCES (³/₄ CUP) SALTED SUNFLOWER SEEDS
³/₄ CUP CHOPPED WALNUTS

Put in blender:

6 OUNCES GRAPEFRUIT JUICE
¹/₂ CUP CORN OIL

Start blender and add gradually:

1 CUP HONEY (PASTEURIZED — THAT RAW STUFF IS DANGEROUS).

Tip: If you leave a little corn oil in the measuring cup, the honey will pour right out without sticking.

Blend well. Turn on oven to 275°F and let it preheat while you add liquid mixture to oat mixture and *STIR.* Mix with a wooden spoon until each oat grain is coated. Then mix some more. This is important!

Bake 1 hour. Stir once after 30 minutes and again at the end of the hour. Then add:

16 OUNCES GRAPENUTS
¹/₂ POUND RAISINS

Mix well and bake another 30 minutes. Don't let the oven temperature go over 275°F, especially after adding the raisins. Stir, cool and package in freezer bags. There are no preservatives; this granola must be kept in the freezer or refrigerator. Makes 4 quarts.

———————

Margaret Searles of Grover Beach, California, grew up in Tillamook, Oregon, and returns to the Oregon coast at every opportunity. Her stories, humor pieces, and articles have appeared in such publications as Bobbin, Whispering Willow Mystery Magazine, PIE, New Times, and In Our Own Voices, and SLO Death, both anthologies. She has written three mystery novels (still, alas, unpublished) and holds memberships in Oregon Writers Colony and Sisters in Crime.

A Letter to My
Cooking-Impaired Daughter

Dear Jacqueline,
Here's a recipe for:

Mediterranean Chicken & Wild Rice
(Inspired by a Salad I Ate at the Heathman Pub and Guessed at
the Ingredients Thinking It Would be Terrific as a Hot Dish)

*1 CUP REALLY HIGH QUALITY WILD RICE BLEND (OR MAKE YOUR OWN WITH
EQUAL PORTIONS OF WILD AND BROWN RICE)*
WASH rice. In a heavy pan with lid — or a **mother** of a casserole
dish — put in rice, 1 large *CHICKEN BOUILLON CUBE, A DOLLOP OF
BUTTER,* and *2 GENEROUS CUPS OF WATER.* Bring to a boil, reduce heat
to simmer, cover with a tight lid, and leave it alone. About 45
minutes later, remove the pan from heat and leave it alone. Come
back 10 minutes later and do the following:

Prepare *1 CUP QUICK-COOKING BROWN RICE* (or white but brown is
better) according to directions. Microwave is okay here. Add this
to the wild rice.

***These first two parts you can do ahead, like the night before
your dinner, and add the rest of the stuff an hour or so before
dinner the next day.***

Okay. You have the pot of rice handy.

1 CUP OF DRIED APRICOTS, SLIVERED. Slice (or sliver — a more
interesting word) apricots until you have about a cup. Into the pot.

1 CUP CURRANTS OR YELLOW RAISINS. Into the pot.

A good *COUPLE OF HANDFULS OF SLICED* (slivered? No.) *CELERY* that
have all those dreadful strings removed. Use your potato peeler.
Into the pot. Not the potato peeler, the celery.

1 CUP OF CHOPPED NUTS. Filberts are good but might be better
toasted in butter and served on fudge ice cream. Slivered (!)
almonds are very good. Walnuts, so, so. Into the pot.

Sometimes I add *1 CUP OF CHOPPED DATES,* depending on my mood.
But then, some folks don't like dates, so I leave them out. Russ
can't eat nuts, so I leave them out and put dates in. Where was I?

Oh yes, the CHICKEN!

Figure one half a breast per person and one half breast for the pot. (This is beginning to sound sexy.) So with this amount of rice, I'd probably buy *3 LARGE CHICKEN BREASTS* which have been boned, skinned and all those fat globs pulled off. This is more expensive to buy but the results are worth it. Depending on your pocketbook, you can get away with less chicken if you add more celery. More things for teeth to crunch on, dontcha know. (Grandpa used to call Aunt Minnie's spaghetti, "airplane spaghetti" because she just held the ground beef and swished it in the air over the top of the pasta.) Use a nice large skillet or frying pan. A little *OLIVE OIL*, please. Wash the chicken and smell it. No smell? That means it's good. Pat those puppies dry with paper towels so the oil doesn't spatter and burn your nose. Sauté, which means fry on low heat, so they turn a nice golden brown. I usually sauté one side, then the other, then put a lid on them for about 10 minutes so they cook through. When they are done, let them cool a bit so you can handle them. You want to cut them into nice big-bite-size chunks. Into the pot.

Dissolve another *LARGE CHICKEN BOUILLON* into *2 CUPS OF BOILING WATER.* Bouillon cubes are very salty so you want to correct seasonings at the last. You may taste now, if you promise not to taste and then stir with the same spoon. Sometimes in this spot, I stir in *2 SPOONSFUL OF BROWN SUGAR.* Some days the dried fruit is sweeter than other days, so fiddle around a bit until it tastes good to you. If it's too sweet, shake in a *SHAKE OR 2 OF VINEGAR*, balsamic is best. If the dish looks too dry, add some water. It should have a little liquid at the bottom of the pan or else it will be too dry after baking. The rice will absorb a ton of liquid. Put this in the oven at about 350°F for about 30 minutes. Lift the lid and give her another stir, and put it back in for another 10 minutes or so while you make a terrific green salad, and slice the French bread.

This recipe makes enough for four to six healthy adults with some left over for lunch the next day. Bon appetit and blessings,

Mama

———◆———

Sally Ann Stevens is a poet, writer and teacher whose work has been published in Pebbles, In Our Own Voices, *and* The American Poetry Anthology *among others. She recently won a first place nonfiction award in* New Millennium Writings, *a Tennessee literary journal.*

Brenda's Company Casserole

BROWN 2 CUPS OF GROUND BEEF:
>Brenda made mud pies in her back yard
>and set them in the sun to bake.

CHOP 1 LARGE ONION:
>The thorns of the blackberry bush
>caught her dress
>She hissed at the bush and cried.

CHOP HALF A GREEN PEPPER:
>Brenda went wading in her pool.
>She played great shark
>and wouldn't let the neighbor kids in.

CHOP 2 CELERY STALKS:
>She climbed her favorite tree.
>Her throne a cool thick limb.
>Her scepter an apple on a branch
>above her head.

SLICE 7 MUSHROOMS:
>Brenda hid under the porch
>like a cat and pounced
>on the ants in the dust.

COMBINE WITH TOMATO SAUCE:
>At the party Brenda won
>every game.
>Even though her eyes
>were "really truly covered"
>she pinned the tail where it belonged
>every time.

SALT AND PEPPER TO TASTE:
>If you don't like it,
>don't tell Brenda.

Judith Massee is a prize winning poet and partner in Media Weavers publishing company. She currently writes the poetry column for the Writers Northwest literary quarterly.

Normally Without Measurements

SINCE THIS IS A RECIPE I normally do without measure ments, feel free to alter to taste. If the recipe looks too dry as you cook it, add more wine, not more soy. If you prefer foods spicy, add more red pepper; if you prefer food sweet, add more basil. Vegetables may be mixed, changed, altered. This combination seems to end up yielding the freshest taste.

Pasta Primavera a la Rusch

3 TABLESPOONS OLIVE OIL
2 CLOVES GARLIC, MINCED
1 TEASPOON DRIED BASIL
1/8 TEASPOON BLACK PEPPER
1/8 TEASPOON CRUSHED RED PEPPER
1/4 TEASPOON SALT OR TO TASTE
6 GREEN ONIONS, SLICED
1 CUP SLICED MUSHROOM
3 TABLESPOONS SOY SAUCE
3 TABLESPOONS WHITE WINE
1 BUNCH ASPARAGUS, CUT INTO BITE-SIZED PIECES
2 FRESH TOMATOES, SLICED
1/2 CUP SHREDDED PARMESAN CHEESE
1 PACKAGE FRESH ANGEL HAIR PASTA, COOKED

Over medium heat, warm olive oil, then add spices, green onions, and mushrooms. Cook 2-3 minutes or until mushrooms have absorbed the olive oil. Add wine, soy sauce and asparagus. Cook until asparagus is tender and bright green, about five minutes maximum. Add tomatoes; cook 30 seconds. Add parmesan cheese; toss with angel hair pasta and serve immediately.

Kristine Kathryn Rusch is the author of many Star Trek novels, including the best-selling The New Rebellion. *Recently, she published the third book in her Fey series,* The Rival. *She has written many other fantasy and science fiction stories. She won the 1994 Hugo award for her work as editor of The Magazine of Fantasy and Science Fiction. She has also been editor of Pulphouse. In 1990, she won the J. W. Campbell award for best new writer.* Gallery of His Dreams *won the 1992 Best Novella award from Locus Magazine.*

The Starlite Drive-in

I WASN'T THERE WHEN THEY DUG UP THE BONES at the old drive-in theater, but I heard about them within the hour. Irma Schmidt phoned Aunt Bliss and delivered the news with such volume that her voice carried across the kitchen to where I was sitting.

After hanging up the receiver, Aunt Bliss peered at me through her thick bifocals. "With all those farms around there, they could be the bones of some animal."

I picked up the coffee mug, drained it, then set it on the worn Formica table. "They could be."

Pursing her lips, she stared hard at me. "I know what you're thinking, but more than one person disappeared that summer."

"Yes," I said, reflectively, "that's true." But my heart was beating faster.

I walked over to the sink, rinsed my cup and tipped it upside down on the drainboard next to a bowl of peaches. My aunt had lived in this house ever since I could remember. I didn't need to look at the linoleum patch to know a hand pump had once jutted from the floor, or at the white wooden cabinets to remember they concealed pulldown bins of flour and sugar. I could almost smell all the peach pies and cobblers she'd baked here the summer before I turned thirteen. With the memories rushing back, I reached for my handbag and car keys.

Aunt Bliss blinked owlishly. "You don't have to go out there, child. Leave it be."

— *from* The Starlite Drive-in, *1997, William Morrow*

Frey Workshop Chicken Pilaf

3 10¹/₂-OUNCE CANS OF CONDENSED CREAM OF MUSHROOM SOUP (UNDILUTED)
3³/₄ CUPS BOILING WATER
¹/₄ CUP DRY SHERRY
1¹/₂ ENVELOPES DRY ONION SOUP MIX
4 CUPS LONG GRAIN WHITE RICE
6 TABLESPOONS CHOPPED CANNED PIMIENTO
15 OR SO PIECES OF CHICKEN (BREASTS AND THIGHS)
BUTTER (OPTIONAL)
SALT AND PEPPER
PAPRIKA
BROCCOLI (OPTIONAL)

In a 4-5 quart casserole, combine first 6 ingredients. Brush chicken with butter; season with salt, pepper and paprika and place on top of rice mixture. Cover. Bake at 375°F for 1¹/₄ hours or until chicken and rice are tender. During the last 10-15 minutes add several handfuls of broccoli if you like. Serve when the whole business is tender.

Feeds about 20 normal people or 15 Rockaway Beach eaters.

———◆———

Marjorie Reynolds began Starlite Drive-in, *with the excerpt above, writing much of this novel at the Colonyhouse. She was born in Indiana, the setting of* Starlite Drive-in. *The recipe is a Jim Frey workshop favorite that she'd fix when it was her turn to cook. Marjorie lives with her family on Mercer Island, Washington, and is hard at work on another novel.*

[175]

My Refrigerator Was Never Pristine

As we bought our new refrigerator, my husband touched the top and said, "Oh look, it comes with dust. You won't have to apply it when we get home."

It was a dirty remark, the only dingy thing about my own Mr. Clean. We were mismatched from the first. He went around writing the date in the mantel dust. I spent the day painting, reading, at a museum, doing anything but housework, then sprayed Lemon Pledge on the wine cabinet in the front hall so it would smell clean as he came in the door. Sometimes it worked, especially if some of the furniture polish got on the tiles and made them a little slippery. With luck, if the light was dim, he might even think I'd waxed.

The problem was never resolved. I did learn to cook. I only once made the mistake of using cucumbers to make a sauteed zucchini dish. They do look alike. The problem with the chocolate chip cookies that could be used for salt licks, well that really wasn't my fault. The little white granules look alike, and I swear somebody switched canisters.

I improved. I always had lots of fresh cilantro. I tossed it with salad, cooked it in the soup, and chopped it for the salsa. But my refrigerator was never pristine. Things tended to get piled up on it as well as in it. If something inside looked green and wasn't in the vegetable compartment, I never fed it to the family. If anything moved, it went down the disposal. Still, when my husband visited me in the hospital and said he cleaned the refrigerator, I begged the doctor to let me stay in another couple days. It would take that long for Mr. Clean to be warmer than the appliance he'd cleaned.

A friend told me she and her husband had much better, (read more serious) things to argue about than the condition of the refrigerator. Maybe so, but I suspect more marriages are endangered by "Odd Couple" patterns of living than infidelity.

We made accommodations. I fastened his socks together with diaper pins so they wouldn't get lost in the wash. I sent his shirts to the cleaners so they would be acceptably pressed. His study was always kept dusted and vacuumed. I never gave anyone food poisoning. But my refrigerator was never pristine.

Refrigerator Rolls

(OK, I cheated, this is not really a recipe)

USE A RECIPE FOR YEAST DOUGH MADE WITH WATER (not milk), so it can be refrigerated up to 5 days. After mixing dough, round up and *BUTTER* the top, cover with plastic wrap and top with a damp towel. When you're ready to bake a portion of the dough, punch that portion down and add extra ingredients, like *NUTS, CHOPPED ONIONS,* or *HERBS.* Shape and let rise until doubled.

Someone once said if they made a perfume that smelled like bread fresh from the oven, it would be a male attractor like none other. The advantage here is that you go to the major trouble once and have fresh bread for several days with little mess or bother.

Add some *CHOPPED PEPPERS* (cilantro and jalepeños if you're brave), some *ONIONS* and you'll have great rolls to go with Variation Two of the following recipe . . . .

Easy Oven Baked Eggs

Use non-stick muffin tins or spray with a non-stick spray. Or use bright cupcake baking cups that go with your china.

VARIATION ONE

Sauté *SHALLOTS AND MUSHROOMS* and put a little in the bottom of each cup. Cook 'til still limp and put *1 STRIP OF BACON* (or breakfast strip) around the inside of the cup. Break *1 MEDIUM SIZE EGG* into each cup. Top with *1 TEASPOON EACH OF SHERRY AND CREAM.*

Bake at 350°F for 15 minutes. Sprinkle with *A LITTLE PARSLEY.*

VARIATION TWO

Sauté *ONIONS AND GREEN PEPPERS,* proceed as above. Cook *TORTILLAS* lightly in *BUTTER* 'til soft. Cut into strips and follow directions for bacon above. Break *1 MEDIUM EGG* into each cup. Top with *1 TEASPOON CREAM* and *1/2 TEASPOON MILD SALSA.* Sprinkle with *GRATED YELLOW CHEESE.* Bake at 350°F for 15 minutes. Sprinkle with *CILANTRO.*

Serves as many as you like. It is a great brunch buffet dish.

Susan Zurcher lives in Port Angeles, Washington. She currently has a contract to complete a screenplay about a vampire for an independent producer and writes about community events for the Peninsula Daily News.

Sanded and Frosted

I PLAYED SICK TO STAY HOME from school on Mamma's birthday. Fourth grade doesn't teach you much, really. But my brother, Jimmy, is in Mamma's sixth grade class and they do science — caving in cans to study air pressure, exploding paper volcanoes, fizzing baking soda with vinegar — good stuff like that.

I do science too, lots of times, but on Mamma's birthday, I played sick to teach myself to cook. I mixed applesauce cake from a box with a smiley lady holding this pretty round cake on a glass cake plate. Making cake wasn't hard at all. I poured the batter into a glass pan and put it in the oven. Then I pushed spoons and all that into the sink so the kitchen would look clean.

Clipper, our spotted spaniel, wiggled his nose for a while. He started in to stretching his muzzle toward the odor of warm butter and applesauce. Clipper quivered, stiff-haired, on point. That meant the cake would be done soon. I needed to make frosting, quick.

On a worn and finger-printy card, Mamma's frosting recipe said "powdered sugar." I searched in all the cupboards. I found all kinds o' sugar, everything from California to Hawaii. I got all these. See? Granulated, confectioner, dark brown, light brown — but powdered? Nothing.

Clipper sniffed, drooping his soft ears through a little pile of cake mix on the floor. Guess I spilled. Clipper licked, you know, like this — his pinky tongue in and out with that slurp-dog sound.

While he did that, I figured what to do about no powdered sugar. If I bought at Fournier's, ol' Pete Fournier would ask what was I doing in his store 'stead of school, like he did to Joey Karstairs.

No way. So, I thought of other things to use — things that might taste like powdered sugar. There aren't many. But — a great idea. I could make powder out of the crystally kind. I could use Daddy's big hammer.

Clipper loped after me, down to the basement. As I reached up for Dad's claw hammer, I noticed this big, flat-faced rubbery kind. It hung way up high on the peg board. I knew I could get more sugar with one blow if I had that flat thing. So I dragged my brothers' sawhorse toward the heavy work table. As I scrambled up, Clipper jumped up. The sawhorse teetered. Clipper landed on the table. I grabbed the light string and quick pushed my knee onto the table. It jabbed into the teeth of an old saw.

I checked. Only a holey nick in my jeans. Didn't even touch skin.

Back upstairs, I whapped my sugar. Grains rolled out from under the rubber hammer. Clipper licked a lot of what spilled, and was still cleaning the floor when Al ran in. He's my big brother, in high school.

"Hi ya, Freckle-face. Whatcha doin'?"

"Nothin'. Making frosting."

"Mom's big day, huh? Smells good."

Al searched for snacks, grains crunched under the soles of his shiny cordovans.

"What's that noise?" He checked his shoe bottoms. "That sugar?"

"Yeah. But not powdered yet."

He glanced at me, and down at the sugar grains. "Swell, he nodded. "I'll be out in the drive, B-ball."

Clipper, tongue out, followed Al's peanut butter sandwich outside.

I was tired of hammering. Instead, I made frosting with unpowdered. The cake was all nice and warm, but pieces of cake trailed along after my frosting knife. Mostly though, I got the lumps covered before everybody got home.

While Daddy and the boys set up a picnic in the back yard, I helped Mamma make salad and she cooked southern-fried.

After dinner, we sang. Mamma blew out her candles.

I took a bite of my cake and chewed on buttered grains. Sugar hadn't melted in like I thought. I hoped no one noticed.

"It's nice to have someone make your birthday cake for you," said Mamma, softly.

I looked around at the flower garden so nobody would see me feeling proud.

"It tastes real good," Dad commented. "Is that butter cream frosting?"

"Well, there's butter," I answered. "No cream though."

Then Al shoveled in his first bite. Too big. His nose turned all red. He pulled his mouth sort of tight, like he was trying to swallow something that tickled.

"Alan Scott!" Mamma sounded real firm. "Swallow!"

He got it down okay and sat there just wiping at his eyes. Clipper's worried brows followed the motion of Jimmy's fork from plate to garden and back.

Jimmy grinned and sang out, "I like eating birthday cake outdoors."

"Yeah," chimed in old Al. "In fact, today it kinda reminds me of eatin' cake at the beach in a high wind."

Jimmy snorted. Al's face turned red. Jimmy's mouth closed up tight. I glanced down at sunlight broken into colors by sugar crystals. With my tongue, I tested and found sweet, buttery... grit....

I think I laughed first — laughed so hard my cake rolled off. Jimmy burst out, then Alan. With tears on their cheeks, Mamma and Daddy held on tight.

"I love you, darlin'," Mamma said, wiping her eyes. "And I'm never going to forget this birthday."

Laughing felt good. Clipper licked up my cake, sand frosting and all. He grinned at me, too — then drooled.

Sour Cream and Applesauce Cake

1/2 CUP BUTTER
1 CUP SUGAR
1/4 CUP SOUR CREAM
1 EGG
3/4 CUP APPLESAUCE

DRY INGREDIENTS
2 CUPS CAKE FLOUR
1/2 TEASPOON SALT
1/2 TEASPOON BAKING POWDER
1 TEASPOON BAKING SODA
1/4 TEASPOON NUTMEG
3/4 TEASPOON CINNAMON
1/2 TEASPOON CLOVES
1 TEASPOON ALLSPICE
1 CUP RAISINS
1/2 CUP CHOPPED WALNUTS

In a small bowl, cream butter, sugar and sour cream. Add egg and applesauce. Beat thoroughly.

Into a separate bowl, sift flour, add other dry ingredients, sift a second time. Add sifted mixture to sugar mixture. Add nuts and raisins. Pour into greased floured 9" loaf pan and bake at

350-375°F for 35 minutes, or until a toothpick stuck in the middle comes out clean.

By the way, no hammering on the counter while the cake cools.

SOUR CREAM FROSTING

2 TABLESPOONS BUTTER
2 TABLESPOONS SOUR CREAM
2 CUPS POWDERED SUGAR

In the top of a double boiler, mix ingredients until smooth. For a more finished flavor, set uncooked frosting over hot water for 15 minutes. Beat again to cool before spreading on cake.

Rae Richen is obviously the Chef de Resistable. Her brothers do occasionally accept invitations for dinner, but only if it is pot luck. They bring dessert. Rae writes great fiction, but this cake was not fiction. It was hard-boiled and gritty truth. Rae is also the author of a history, To Serve Those Most in Need, *the story of the West Coast's largest social service agency, Albertina Kerr Centers.*

Stove's Fault

This not for the faint of heart, it could give Betty Crocker gray hair before her time. Martha Stewart would not think it "A GOOD THING!"

I was a teenager, bored with summer, and in charge of younger siblings. Mom told me to make blackberry jam while she was gone for the day. Our kitchen was hot from the wood burning range. I do recall reading the step by step directions on the back of a brown liquid pectin bottle, crush berries, add sugar, add pectin, etc. I put the kettle on the hot part of stove and settled down with a "Ranch Romance" magazine. It was late afternoon before I remembered the jam, hid the magazine and filled the jars.

That winter when a jar of jam was opened, my brother made a production out of removing jam for his toast, and said the knife broke. I though he was kidding until I grabbed the jar and found I had invented some new type of plastic.

All the tormenting about what did you do to the jam was countered with, "Hey! It's not my fault, it's The Stove's Fault!"

I do have a great recipe to share that is a winner and no one will fault you.

This recipe is from a gal from Jamaica, West Indies, who lived with our family though an exchange program.

Banana Curls

A great appetizer. Wonderful blend of flavors. Easy.

Cut PEELED RIPE BANANAS in half lengthwise, then into fourths. Roll banana pieces in a cinnamon sugar mixture. (*1 TEASPOON CINNAMON* to 1/2 *CUP SUGAR*). Wrap bananas with 1/2 *SLICE OF RAW BACON*, put a toothpick through to secure, spear an *ORANGE SECTION* on toothpick and broil 10 minutes on a cookie sheet, or until bacon is done.

Irene Emmert was born to write. She can't recall when she wasn't writing, be it letters, thoughts, diaries or stories. Ideas float and mull in her thoughts — humorous, serious and silly things. Her everyday life experiences would be a best seller. So many thoughts . . . so little time.

Dinner Sauce

"And who is Steve?" I ask. My spouse recites several pertinent facts about the man he would invite to dinner — class of ... University of ... keynote speaker at .... We compare weekly planners, flag a Friday. "Dinner guest, concert," I chirp, "nice evening."

I thumb through menus — spaghetti. You can't go wrong with spaghetti — stock my cupboards several days ahead, then swing into high gear the morning of the engagement. With the right proportions of lean, browned, ripe, chopped ingredients simmering in my well-seasoned iron skillet, I run non-stop through an agenda of necessary (as I perceive them) pre-dinner activities.

I scrub, dust or vacuum every square foot of living space in my home. There's the dog to walk, cat and kitty tray to tuck in the basement, new garbage can liner under the sink.

There's best china and crystal, linen table napkins instead of save-the-earth recycled paper ones, salad, garlic bread, dessert. Add to this the usual fussing around with hair, make-up and finding something — I don't know what — to wear. Add to this Dick hovering about hoping to be useful, I start to feel a bit harried as the clock hand races through countdown.

Blastoff! Six o'clock sharp. The doorbell rings. It would be nice, we have hinted to our guest, if we could eat promptly at six for an early start to the concert. So while Dick invites Steve to "please come in" exactly on the appointed hour, I give a last look around my country kitchen.

Country kitchen means, among other things, tidying up the kitchen before guests arrive. My sterling place settings and cooking arena are a dish cloth throw apart; anything not washed, washed up after or put away becomes part of the dining ambiance.

I am pleased with the big dual purpose room: a vase of fresh cuttings graces the tea cart, lamps add a nice touch, candles highlight the sparkle of long-stemmed goblets. Kitchen counters are crumb and smear free. All preliminary pots, cups, knives and spoons are washed and put away. I glance in the mirror of our polished old buffet; no hint of my mounting stress. The dog sleeps on his freshly laundered bed cover. Culinary redolence emanates through the doorways; house smells wonderful.

"Hi Steve." I extend my hand to the tall, casual-mannered gentleman living up, every whit, to my expectations. "We'll have plenty of time to visit before heading to the concert" (I continue to fret about unreserved seating). Something like "I'm really looking forward to . . ." from Steve. A few more cordial greetings and affirmations while jockeying by the front door. . . . The evening whips graciously past milepost two.

Dick hangs Steve's coat in my immaculate hall closet, and ushers our guest into my spotless living room while I excuse myself back to the food. At ten minutes after six, I remove the pert but useless handkerchief-sized apron I was careful to be wearing when I met Steve in the foyer, pat my blown-dry hairdo, glide into the living room and announce to the two men still skirting the edge of good conversation that we are ready to eat.

"Buffet style," I gush, as I ease our visitor toward the kitchen, trying desperately to remember if I put a fresh bar of soap in the bathroom. "We're casual here, just help yourself." Steve says how hungry he is, how great it smells. Dick says how hungry he is, and that it does, indeed, smell delicious. I say just make yourself at home and dig right in.

With Steve and spouse waiting to do exactly that, I remove the heavy lid from my sauce skillet, savor the surge of aromatic steam. A roomy spoon rests picturesquely on its blue and white concave rooster. As I drop the serving utensil into my bubbly brew, something niggles at me. A tight smile while I scan the table: salad, dressing, bread — it's all there. So what's wrong?

At the precise moment when Steve is prevailed upon to serve himself, it hits me. As in a dream, I hear Dick urge our guest to "eat up, there's plenty of everything." I forgot the pasta.

Pasta Sauce sans Pasta

GROUND BEEF (*1 POUND*)
ONION (*1 MEDIUM DICED*)
GREEN PEPPER (*½ DICED*)
PREPARED SPAGHETTI SAUCE (*⅓ JAR*)
TOMATO SAUCE (*16 OUNCES*)
GARLIC (*2 CLOVES MINCED*)
PARSLEY, OREGANO, SAGE, SALT, PEPPER, THYME, BASIL, BAY LEAF, PAPRIKA,
    CHILI POWER (*PROVERBIAL PINCHES OF THIS AND THAT TO TASTE*)
WORCESTERSHIRE SAUCE (*2 TABLESPOONS*)
CATSUP (*COUPLE DASHES*)

Simmer — simmer — simmer.

———————◆———————

A native of North Carolina, Carol Ann Lantz has lived in the forested foothills north of Corvallis, Oregon, for the last 24 years. She received a bachelor of science degree from Oregon State University in botany, and did graduate work in plant physiology. Her interests, outside of being a wife and homemaker, include almost any aspect of out-of-doors, music and creative writing, especially poetry.

Erma's Surprise

I'm through cleaning in the living room, why don't you sit in here awhile, Erma?"

That's Tina, the girl who comes in twice a week to help me. She knows I can't get down on that low furniture. I wish to God I *could* sit in there. These straight kitchen chairs feel like steel rods against my back, and my not-so-dainty butt hangs over the edges. And the TV's on a shelf higher than my head, so I feel like someone looking for the big dipper when I watch it — giving me a nonstop crick in my neck.

The problem is, she's 25 and doesn't understand being 68 and having weak lungs, a failing heart and living in a flypaper mobile home that's blessed with one shelf and not enough room for a lousy TV stand.

Next she'll say, "I don't know how one person can get a house so dirty." And I'll say, "I can barely walk to the bathroom to pee. How can I get a house dirty."

In the middle of "The Price Is Right," Tina walks in gathering ashtrays. One by one she tips them over the trash can and gives them a little shake and says, "ewe," like a sick kitten. She never washes them. Says they stink so bad she can barely touch them. Hell, if she washed them once in a while they wouldn't stink.

I take a long drag from my cigarette and exhale as she walks by. She waves a prissy hand across her face, but says nothing.

And my stomach, sounding like an electric grinder, is getting on my nerves. I haven't eaten since yesterday's meals-on-wheels. I don't cook anymore. I get too short of breath. And if I stand very long my feet balloon over my house-shoes like mushroom caps.

Usually, I have soup or frozen dinners for my evening meal, but I'm out of money and my check won't come for three more days.

As "The Price Is Right" ends, Tina opens the refrigerator and heaves out a covered plastic bowl big enough to hold three meals; and a bag full of lettuce — the dark leafy kind that has a nice crunch to it. Oh, sure, she's going to eat. She's worked up one hell of an appetite vacuuming and emptying ashtrays. But let's give her a little credit. She also swished the toilet and fluttered the dust rag.

Now I want to watch *"Court TV,"* but the scraping of food from bowl to plate is distracting. And my stomach sounds like thunder

and feels like there's a chain saw plowing through it. I light
another cigarette.

As I exhale, Tina, holding two plates of food, turns and sets
one of them in front of me. I stare, speechless as a dunce, for
several seconds.

"Thought you might like some chicken salad. I'll put what's left
in your refrigerator so you can have some tomorrow . . . if you'd
like." She sits across from me. "I call it Chicken Salad Surprise."

"Well, yes, that would be nice." I scoop up a large bite and my taste buds ache from disuse. Soon, I'm eating like someone shoveling snow.

When I finally look up Tina's watching me. I lay my fork down, burp, wipe my mouth with the napkin she put by my plate and search my mind for something stunning to say. And she's still staring like she's never seen anyone eat before.

Finally, I say, "There's some hard rolls in the freezer that might go with this . . . chicken . . . surprise."

"Well, they certainly would," says Tina and she grabs them from the freezer and pops them into the microwave.

But I want you to know, I didn't offer my bread to be nice, necessarily. I just wanted her to stop staring at me.

Chicken Salad Surprise

2 CUPS DICED COOKED CHICKEN
1 STALK CELERY, CHOPPED
1 8½-OUNCE CAN CRUSHED PINEAPPLE, DRAINED
2 TABLESPOONS SLICED PIMENTO-STUFFED OLIVES
½ CUP MAYONNAISE
DASH OF SALT
LEAF LETTUCE
¼ CUP CHOPPED CASHEWS

Combine chicken, celery, pineapple and olives. Add mayonnaise and salt. Toss lightly. Chill. To serve, place lettuce leaves on plates. Spoon salad over lettuce; sprinkle with cashews. Makes 4 servings.

———————◆———————

Valetta Smith is a registered nurse working in home health and hospice. She has written short stories and essays and is working on both a mystery and a mainstream novel about three couples facing midlife challenges.

Index of Authors

Index of Recipes

About Colonyhouse

Colonyhouse is owned by Oregon Writers Colony (OWC), a not-for-profit community of writers dedicated to helping writers grow in their craft. It is used by critique groups, workshops and individuals. Colonyhouse is a beach house with "a 20-foot riverstone fireplace rising into an open beam cathedral ceiling, hand-hewn log walls, carved wooden door handles and a staircase crafted of naturally shaped wood. Light flows in from generous windows framing the turbulence of the Pacific to the west and the serenity of Lake Lytle to the east." — *Jessica Wade*

Conferences and workshops. In addition to an annual spring weekend conference in Newport, Oregon, OWC offers workshops at Colonyhouse and in the Portland, Oregon, metro area. A fall conference near Portland is under consideration.

Pick Me Up Tuesdays. These informal early-evening gatherings in the Portland, Oregon, metro area include topics such as critique groups, the writer's life, journaling, and authors reading their published work.

Publications. Three editions of the anthology, *In Our Own Voices*, have been edited by Elizabeth Bolton and published by the Colony. The 1997 edition is still in print and available for purchase. The Colonygram, OWC's bimonthly newsletter for members, includes articles on writing, "Publishers Weekly" updates, writing by members and information about OWC events. A world wide web site is maintained with scheduled conferences and workshops posted at www.teleport.com/~witch/owc/owc.htm>.

Ordering information

Purchase of this book is an investment in support of the Colonyhouse which nourishes writers' spirits.

To order cookbooks or anthologies, write to: Publications, Oregon Writers Colony, PO Box 15200, Portland OR, 97293-5200. Make checks payable to Oregon Writers Colony and include your name, address, zip code, and daytime phone number.

Seasoned with Words: Stories, Memoirs and Poems About Food. $22.00 a book, plus $3.00 shipping and handling. For more than two, add $2.00 for each additional cookbook.

In Our Own Voices. $10.50 plus $1.50 shipping and handling. For more than two, add $1.00 for each additional anthology.